MARY QUEEN
OF SCOTS

MARY QUEEN OF SCOTS

Nancy Lotz and Carlene Phillips

MORGAN REYNOLDS

PUBLISHING

Greensboro, North Carolina

European Queens

Eleanor of Aquitaine
Elizabeth I
Queen Isabella
Catherine the Great
Marie Antoinette
Queen Victoria
Catherine de' Medici
Mary Queen of Scots

MARY QUEEN OF SCOTS

Copyright © 2007 by Nancy Lotz and Carlene Phillips

Library of Congress Cataloging-in-Publication Data

Lotz, Nancy, 1945-
  Mary, Queen of Scots / by Nancy Lotz and Carlene Phillips. -- 1st ed.
    p. cm. -- (European queens)
  Includes bibliographical references and index.
  ISBN-13: 978-1-59935-040-0
  ISBN-10: 1-59935-040-8
  1. Mary, Queen of Scots, 1542-1587. 2. Scotland--History--Mary Stuart,
1542-1567. 3. Great Britain--History--Elizabeth, 1558-1603. 4. Queens--Scot-
land--Biography. I. Phillips, Carlene, 1938- II. Title.
  DA787.A1L68 2007
  941.105092--dc22
  [B]
                                        2006101091

Printed in the United States of America
First Edition

To all the young readers who will come to learn more about themselves by knowing history

Contents

Mary Queen of Scots
Heritage Images

1

Rough Wooing

Mary Stewart never knew her father. When she was born at Linlithgow Palace, near Edinburgh, on December 8, 1542, James V, King of Scotland, lay dying seventeen miles away at Falkland Palace. James had been taken to Falkland by his attendants after the English forces of Henry VIII had decimated his army at the battle of Solway Moss. Twelve thousand of his men had been killed or captured at the battle, including twenty-three powerful nobles that Henry had taken back to London and imprisoned.

After losing the battle, James had seemed to lose his will to live. He fell ill and never recovered. The men gathered around his death bed later reported that when James received word of his daughter's birth he mumbled, "It cam wi' a lass,

King James V of Scotland, Mary's father

and will gang [go] wi' a lass." His cryptic remark referred to the beginning of the reign of the House of Stewart—the family had come to the throne when a daughter of the legendary Robert the Bruce married Walter Stewart early in the fourteenth century. Now James was predicting the Stewart dynasty would end with a woman—his newborn daughter Mary. When the king's attendants urged him to bless his daughter, he refused. Six days later, on December 14, he turned his face to the wall and died.

Marie de Guise

After her husband's death, Mary's mother, the French born Marie de Guise, had little energy to spend grieving. Grief had already exhausted her. Marie had given birth to a son named Robert less than a year before, but the baby had lived only two days. Then, only a few days later, her older son, James, died just days short of his first birthday. Marie had grieved for her sons throughout her third pregnancy. Now she had another child, a fragile newborn girl born prematurely, who was suddenly next in line to inherit a besieged throne.

Before the baby Mary could become queen, she had to survive, and that would be up to her grieving mother. Fortunately, Marie was soon able to take delight in her new baby, who had smooth, creamy skin and fair features. If she continued to thrive, the little princess, who was named after her mother and the Virgin Mary, would be a beauty.

Outside Linlithgow Palace, Scotland seemed to be coming apart. The Scottish monarchy, though ostensibly the center of power in the kingdom, lacked control over the nobles, who were primarily concerned with their own interests. James V and his predecessors had not been able to follow the example set by the Tudors in England. There, Henry VII, the first Tudor king, had steadily reduced the number and the power of the English nobility in the early years of his reign and eventually had forced them to swear loyalty to him.

The Stewart dynasty had been in a precarious position for decades. Beginning in the fourteenth century, a series of minor children had inherited the throne. In each case, a regent had been appointed to govern the country until the child came of age. These long interims without a monarch in power had allowed the nobility to accumulate more than enough power and wealth to challenge any king. In Scotland, the nobility's primary

Henry VII of England was the first Tudor king. *(Courtesy of Bridgeman Art Library)*

allegiance was to their families and local regions. The worst thing that could happen, from their view, was for one family, or king or queen, to accumulate too much power. This led to ceaseless feuds, wars, and revolts. Even the noble families allied with the Stewarts used the regencies to increase their own power. Threats also came from the "auld enemy" to the south: England. England had long wanted to take control of Scotland and had invaded many times over the centuries. At the beginning of the sixteenth century, King Henry VII of England had tried a different tactic when he convinced James IV of Scotland to marry his daughter, Margaret Tudor. But despite this attempt to unite the royal families, the strife and tension continued.

The tension was exacerbated by the fact that England had long been enemies with France, while France was Scotland's strongest ally. When Henry VIII became the English king in 1509 he was determined to control Scotland and to rid it of French influence. Henry VIII professed his belief in an English saying, "Who that intendeth France to win, with Scotland let him begin."

Another source of conflict, and one that would play a significant part in Mary's life, was the schism between Protestants and Catholics that began early in the sixteenth century. What came to be called the Protestant Reformation permanently altered Christianity in Europe. The divisions began on theological grounds, but quickly became political, as secular rulers began lining up either in support of the Catholic Church, or one of the new Protestant faiths.

When Mary became queen, the Scottish National Church was still officially Catholic, but it was being torn apart and would soon give way to Protestantism. Some Scots thought

Early map of
Scotland, England
and France (*The
University of Texas*)

the Catholic Church was more interested in accumulating wealth than in serving the needs of its believers. The Catholic Church owned approximately half the land in Scotland, and many, especially powerful nobles, began to question why it should be so wealthy. There were also questions and a growing disillusionment with the doctrine of the Catholic Church, which had held sway over the vast majority of Christians in Western Europe for more than a thousand years.

A different religious revolution had occurred in England. King Henry VIII broke from the Catholic Church when the pope refused to grant him a divorce from his wife, the Spanish princess Catherine of Aragon. Henry wanted to divorce

Henry VIII, king of England, attempted to arrange a marriage between Mary Stewart and his son Edward.

Catherine because she had not produced a male heir, but the pope was not able to grant the divorce because Catherine was related to the powerful Hapsburg family. Henry would not be dissuaded and had set his sights on another woman at court, Anne Boleyn, to be his next queen. Henry broke with the Catholic Church in 1531 and created the Church of England, naming himself its leader. This led some Scottish Protestants to look to Henry for support in their struggle against the Catholic Church in Scotland.

Marie de Guise had no intention of allowing Scotland to go the way of England. She remained loyal to the Catholic Church, as did her powerful family back in France, and she intended for her daughter to remain Catholic. Marie had to take the religious and political situation into consideration as she tried to make two immediate decisions—who would rule the country as regent until Mary came of age, and who would be Mary's future husband.

The position of regent carried all the power and responsibility of royal office. There were two main contenders, James Hamilton and Cardinal David Beaton. Hamilton, the Earl of Arran, was an indecisive and self-serving man—Marie de Guise called him "the most inconstant man in the world, for whatsoever he determineth today, he changeth tomorrow." He favored England and Protestantism, and wanted the governorship in order to arrange a marriage between his own son and Mary.

The other contender, Cardinal Beaton, claimed that the king's will named him regent. Beaton had the support of the Catholic nobles and those who wanted to remain independent of England.

Despite his personal weaknesses, Arran was made governor, primarily because of the influence of the nobles captured at the battle of Solway Moss. During their captivity, they had signed agreements with King Henry VIII vowing to support Protestantism in Scotland. When Henry freed them, the nobles, who had also been paid handsome bribes, supported Hamilton, Henry's pick for regent.

The selection of Hamilton was a defeat for Marie, but the question of Mary's future marriage promised to be even more troubling. The betrothal of a queen, even an infant queen, was an international issue. Scotland needed an alliance with a strong foreign power to act as a counterweight to England. Not surprisingly, Henry VIII wanted to arrange a marriage between Mary and his son Edward. This would accomplish his long-standing desire to unite the two countries. Also, because England would be providing the male half of the marriage, it would be the dominant partner in the marriage alliance.

The nobles who had been freed by Henry agreed to help bring about the marriage of Mary and Edward. In July of 1543, they arranged for the Scottish Parliament to sign the Treaty of Greenwich, which agreed to the marriage of Edward and Mary and promised to send the child queen to England when she reached age ten.

Marie de Guise had no intention of letting her only daughter marry the child of Henry VIII. She maintained the pretext of cooperation as a way to stall for time while she sought help from France. When an ambassador of King Henry VIII came from England to check on the health of the baby, Marie showed her off with pride. The ambassador confirmed that he had never seen a more beautiful baby, remarking, "It is as goodly a child as I have seen of her age, and as like to live, with the grace of God."

In the summer of 1543, Marie moved Mary from the beautiful but poorly fortified palace of Linlithgow to Stirling, a castle near the west coast. Stirling was a fortress built high on a rock overlooking the plains. The seven-month-old queen traveled there with an armed escort of more than 3,000 men.

Marie worked to stave off English efforts to take Mary to London earlier than was stipulated in the treaty. Meanwhile, she communicated with her mother and her two Guise brothers, who were highly influential at the French court, to arrange French support.

Marie provided Mary with friends, an education, and plenty of outdoor activities to keep her healthy. Four of Mary's friends were daughters of the four Frenchwomen who had

At the young age of seven months, Mary was moved to Stirling Castle on the west coast of Scotland. *(Library of Congress)*

accompanied Marie to Scotland. Each of the women had married Scotsmen and each had a daughter named Mary. The women and their daughters lived at Stirling and the four young Marys became Mary Stewart's playmates and closest friends. Marie de Guise also brought four of James V's illegitimate children to Stirling, including the eldest, James Stewart, who was twelve years older than Mary. He organized games and took the five Marys sledding on the icy slopes outside the castle, and before long, Mary adored and idolized her older half-brother.

By October 1543, King Henry VIII's influence was waning in Scotland. Arran had proved his inconsistency by switching his allegiance and joining Beaton and the pro-French, pro-Catholic faction. Encouraged by Arran's change, Marie decided the time was right to defy Henry VIII. Although the Treaty of Greenwich forbade Mary from being crowned Queen of Scotland in her own right, Marie arranged her daughter's coronation.

The day of the ceremony dawned clear, but clouds gathered as the day went on and a gray mist filled the air. The infant was carried in a procession from her nursery in the castle to the neighboring Chapel Royal. She was dressed in a red velvet cloak with ermine trim over a jeweled satin gown. Nobles knelt and pledged their loyalty. The Earl of Arran carried the crown, the Earl of Argyll carried the sword, and the Earl of Lennox carried the scepter. As Cardinal Beaton set the crown on Mary's head, the nine-month-old queen let out a cry.

To show their disapproval, the pro-English party did not attend the coronation. Henry VIII's ambassador described the ceremony as simple, "with such solemnity as they do in this country, which is not very costly." Simple though it may have been, the coronation was important—it conferred religious as well as civil legitimacy on Mary.

Soon after the coronation, Henry VIII took his revenge. Henry was furious at Arran's defection and was also upset that the Scottish Parliament had annulled the Treaty of Greenwich, effectively canceling the marriage arrangements. It became clear to Henry that the Scottish nobles had been persuaded by Marie de Guise to favor an alliance with France. He, however, was determined to reinstate the marriage agreement.

Henry began what came to be called his "rough wooing." He ordered an invasion of the Scottish city of Edinburgh and commanded his troops to "put all to fire and the sword, burn Edinburgh town, so razed and defaced when you have sacked and gotten what you can of it as there may remain forever a perpetual memory of the vengeance of God lighted upon [them] for their falsehood and disobedience." Fires raged for three days and, although the Castle of Edinburgh proved impregnable, almost all the houses and churches were destroyed.

The "rough wooing" devastated Scotland. The nobles

blamed Arran for the destruction and began advocating for Marie to become Arran's co-regent. After being appointed co-regent, Marie was given a seat on the Privy Council, the select body of advisors to the monarch, and a seat in Parliament, where she worked to bring Scotland under French protection. When the future King Henry II of France had a son in 1544, Marie began to work on arranging a marriage for Mary with the newborn French heir.

Meanwhile, the religious conflict escalated. Marie's chief advisor, Cardinal Beaton, was often at Stirling. Although Catholic, Beaton did not share Marie's desire for a French marriage for Mary. He worried it would incite a violent attack on the Catholic Church by Scottish Protestants. Rumors spun throughout the land about the Church's greed and corruption. Protestants charged that the Catholic clergy lived off money given to the church by the community, while the truly needy were neglected.

In March 1546, Cardinal Beaton ordered the execution of a Protestant preacher named George Wishart. As Wishart was burned to death, Beaton watched from his castle wall. Three months later, in an act of retaliation, John Knox, a prominent Protestant preacher, and his followers stormed St. Andrews Castle, seized and murdered Beaton, and hung his dismembered body from the castle wall. Knox and his men held St. Andrews for nearly a year. Beaton's murder made it clear to Marie that her only chance to keep the crown for Mary, and to keep Scotland Catholic, was to get French support.

The year 1547 saw the deaths of two great monarchs, King Henry VIII of England and King Francis I of France. In the years after Henry's death, England began a period of uncertainty. His son and heir Edward, who was Protestant, was still a minor and in poor health, and his eldest daughter

Mary was devoted to her mother, Catherine, and her Catholic religion.

In France, the death of Francis I meant that the new king, Henry II, would be under greater pressure to find a suitable bride for his young son, Francis II.

Henry VIII's death did not stop a planned English invasion of Scotland. In an unprecedented display of unity, Scots from all over the country abandoned their old rivalries and gathered to fight the English. When the English troops approached Edinburgh, they were surprised by the largest Scottish army in history, but it soon became clear the English were better trained and equipped. Arran fled the field and his troops panicked. In the Battle of Pinkie Cleugh, 10,000 Scots were killed. Once again the English had killed some of Scotland's finest men—only five years after the battle at Solway Moss.

After the loss, Marie decided that even Stirling Castle was no longer safe. She arranged for the young queen and the four Marys to be taken secretly to Inchmahome Priory, a monastery located on a small island, a few hours ride from Stirling. The island and its buildings, with its trees, ancient walls, and corridors, was an ideal and secure place for the children.

The secrecy of the trip to the island, as well as its mysterious atmosphere and beauty, appealed to Mary. She was now an intelligent child of four and likely aware that she was the center of intrigue. After a few weeks, when Marie decided it was safe, Mary was returned to Stirling, where she remained as Marie completed arrangements for her to leave the country.

Ironically, the devastating defeat at Pinkie Cleugh created

an advantage for Marie because it became clear to many Scots that the only way to remain independent of England was to form an alliance with the French, via an agreement to a French marriage for Mary. Arran, as co-regent, and King Henry II of France signed an agreement promising to defend Scotland and respect its independence. Also, Henry II's most important advisors, Mary's uncles Francis, Duke of Guise and Charles, Cardinal of Lorraine, would negotiate the withdrawal of English soldiers from Scotland. Mary would be sent to the French court and groomed to marry Henry II's son. Only four years and seven months old, Mary was engaged for the second time.

Mary was moved to Dumbarton Castle on the west coast of Scotland to await the galley ship King Henry sent to transport her to France. One Frenchman remarked that she was "one of the most perfect creatures that ever was seen" and with such splendid beginnings "it isn't possible to hope for more from a princess on this earth."

In July 1548, now five and a half, Mary kissed her mother goodbye and walked with her head held high onto the royal galley. She was accompanied by the four Marys. Marie watched from shore as her daughter sailed away. Politically, she knew this was the only solution, but she was torn by a mother's sorrow at losing her only surviving child.

Marie knew that, even with French aid, the situation in Scotland was still dangerous. Rival factions of nobles continued to vie for power, and the religious conflict showed no signs of ending. But Marie was determined to spend the rest of her life keeping the throne of Scotland safe for her daughter until she could rule her country in deed as well as in name.

Most Perfect Child

Five-year-old Mary and her entourage arrived in France in August. For the next ten years, she lived a luxurious childhood. During those years she delighted most everyone she met and was fussed over by her Guise relatives, who were excited that she would be queen of France someday. Most importantly, in the rich, fertile countryside of France, she was no longer at the center of political and religious strife.

Mary's memories of Scotland faded, but Marie had made efforts to ensure her daughter wouldn't forget her homeland. Marie sent a Scottish entourage, both children and adults. The four Marys, a nurse, a governess, and more than one hundred nobles went to the French court with Mary. James Stewart, Mary's seventeen-year-old half brother, whom she had so idolized when he came to Stirling Castle, had also made the crossing with the group and then traveled on to the University of Paris.

It took two months for Mary and her entourage to reach the court of King Henry II. The king was away fighting in Italy and did not return until the fall. During the interim, Mary became well acquainted with her uncles Charles, Cardinal of Lorraine and Francis, Duke of Guise; her grandmother Antoinette, Duchess of Guise; and Diane de Poitiers, the king's mistress.

The Guises were one of the most powerful families in France. As the conflict between French Catholics and Protestants turned into a bitter and bloody civil war, the Guises championed the Catholic side. Mary's two uncles, the duke and the cardinal, grew to love their niece, but they never forgot her political importance. One day she would be the French queen. Her uncles were also mindful that Mary was high in the line of succession to the English throne.

Mary's grandmother, the Duchess Antoinette de Guise, also had great influence. The duchess was an imposing woman and fiercely loyal to her family. She helped manage her husband's vast landholdings as well as the political careers of her sons. She had given birth to twelve children in twenty-one years, an impressive ten of whom survived into adulthood.

Duchess Antoinette was dazzled by Mary's appearance. "She is the prettiest and best for her age that you ever saw," she wrote. "She has auburn hair, with a fine complexion, and I think that when she comes of age she will be a beautiful girl, because her skin is delicate and white." Antoinette was also impressed by Mary's self-assuredness and curiosity.

As pleased as she was with Mary's attractive demeanor, the duchess wanted to change things about the little queen. Antoinette helped Mary grow into an elegant and accomplished princess. When Mary first arrived in France, the duchess determined that her dresses were not elegant enough and her companions were uncouth and "not even as clean as

Diane de Poitiers, a mistress of King Henry, watched over Mary in Henry's absence.

they might be." She wrote to Marie that she wanted to replace Mary's Scottish nurse and governess with Frenchwomen, but Marie had anticipated this and sent instructions that none of her daughter's Scottish attendants were to be dismissed.

Diane de Poitiers, King Henry's mistress, was also frequently at the castle at Saint-Germain where Mary grew up. Diane was a clever, intelligent woman who held a great deal of influence over the king. She even ran the royal household in his absence, and Henry II had left her instructions regarding Mary. He wanted her to share the best bedchamber with his eldest daughter, Elizabeth. He also commanded that Mary was to "walk ahead of my daughters because her marriage to my son is agreed, and on top of that she is a crowned queen." When she heard of these instructions from the king, Antoinette was pleased because it meant King Henry would pay for Mary's expenses, including her servants, clothing, jewelry, and education.

Diane had the four Marys removed to a convent, as Henry had asked. Without her friends to talk to, Mary eventually gave up speaking Scots, a language the French thought vulgar, and perfected her French. Henry considered Mary's position as queen of Scotland secondary to her future role as queen of France.

Mary became more and more the French princess as time passed. Because the French language did not contain the letter "w," Mary even changed the spelling of her family name from Stewart to Stuart. She also used the French form of her name as her signature and wrote it in the French manner, MARIE, with all the letters the same size.

Despite the influence of powerful adults, the most important person at the French court for Mary was her future husband,

Francis, the oldest child of Henry II, was betrothed to Mary at the age of four.

Francis, the son of the House of Valois, and the dauphin, or heir, to the French throne. Francis was the oldest child of Henry II and his queen, the Italian born Catherine de' Medici. Although they were opposites in many ways, Mary and Francis bonded quickly. Henry II later remarked, "From the very first day they met, my son and she got on as well together as if they had known each other for a long time."

Francis was nearly five when almost six-year-old Mary arrived at the court. He was a timid and not particularly intelligent child, while Mary was vivacious, clever, and charming. He was short and physically unattractive; she was tall and pretty. Francis stuttered. Mary spoke with ease. Francis was immediately drawn to Mary, and she seemed to realize he did not have her intelligence and personality and developed a protective affection for him, almost as though he were a younger brother. In the years ahead, Mary and Francis would be together almost constantly.

As a child, Mary spent time with Catherine de' Medici at St. Germain.

In the late fall, when King Henry returned to court, he pronounced that Mary was "the most perfect child that I have ever seen." However, like her uncles, Henry's fondness for Mary did not blind him to the power she held as the future queen of France and Scotland. With the promise of marriage between Mary and Francis, King Henry was assured some measure of control over Scotland. More importantly, with Mary's claim to the English throne, he or his heirs might one day exercise similar control over England, France's longtime enemy.

Henry considered Mary to be next in line for the English throne, behind Mary Tudor, a devout Catholic. Henry II agreed with the papal declaration that Henry VIII's legitimate line ended with Mary Tudor, meaning that Elizabeth, Anne Boleyn's daughter, and Edward, the son Henry bore with yet another wife, were illegitimate and could not inherit the throne. The pope and Henry II thought Mary Stuart should succeed Mary Tudor, and her French uncles encouraged Henry II to pursue her claim to the English throne.

As Mary grew older, Henry remained fond of her. When Mary was about ten years old, one of her uncles reported to Marie: "I can assure you that the King is so delighted with her that he passes much time talking with her, and for an hour together she amuses him with wise and witty conversation, as if she was a woman of twenty-five." Catherine de' Medici was also enchanted by the vivacious child, and Mary spent her first ten years in France basking in loving attention and material luxury.

Although France was imperiled by foreign wars, increasing debt, and religious conflict between the Catholics and the French Protestants, who were called Huguenots, Mary was untouched by these difficulties. Along with Francis and his sisters Elizabeth and Claude, she attended performances by traveling acrobats, actors, singers, and musicians, and enjoyed a variety of pets. Mary was particularly fond of ponies and loved riding. She adopted the Italian fashion of wearing breeches, made of coarse, sturdy material, under her skirts while riding, allowing her to ride astride her horse rather than sidesaddle, as was customary for women. She enjoyed going hunting with Francis and indulged her love of dogs, especially spaniels and terriers; at one point twenty-two lap dogs traveled with the royal household.

Mary's wardrobe was luxurious. She wore gowns of gold damask and dresses cut from red and yellow taffeta, with orange petticoats underneath. Her outfits were embellished with fur, jewels, and delicate embroidery for different occasions and she had pairs and pairs of different colored shoes to choose from, some made of velvet. Each outfit was accompanied by a bonnet and a purse to hold her delicate combs and gilded mirror.

Mary and the other children loved to visit Anet, the home of Diane de Poitiers, which was situated close to Saint-Germain, only a short barge trip from Paris. Young Francis was so enthralled with Anet he wrote about the "beautiful gardens! Beautiful galleries! So many other beauties!" While at Anet, Diane schooled Francis in courtly manners and counseled him in ways to open his heart to his future bride. Francis tried to absorb the lessons. When he was given a suit of armor by Mary's uncles, he called himself a gentle knight trying "to win the heart of the beautiful and honest lady who is your niece." Mary was flattered by his attention and was a willing recipient of the dauphin's child kisses and murmured endearments.

Even though the royal children enjoyed ample material luxuries and leisure activities, Mary's education was taken seriously. Catherine de' Medici, Diane de Poitiers, and the Cardinal of Lorraine chose her tutors. She and the two princesses followed a curriculum almost identical to the dauphin's. They studied classical languages, rhetoric, history, and poetry. When she had mastered the basic skills, Mary joined the dauphin in advanced Latin lessons, where she wrote compositions in the language. At the age of thirteen, she delivered a Latin

Chateau Anet, the home of Diane de Poitiers, where young Mary and Francis enjoyed spending time. *(Courtesy of Bridgeman Art Library)*

declamation defending the education of women in the great hall of the Louvre palace in Paris.

In her Latin essays and speech-giving, Mary exhibited competence, though not brilliance. She liked the French poetry produced by the writers at Henry's court, particularly the verses they wrote for her. She tried her hand at writing her own poems and was a generally attentive student. Francis, on the other hand, had little interest in studying, preferring to ride and hunt.

Religion remained an important part of Mary's everyday life. Her mother had instructed that she attend daily Mass, and her own special communion dishes traveled with her from castle to castle. At the age of twelve Mary took her first Holy Communion. She later referred to it as the happiest day of her life. Mary continued to be a committed Catholic. However, following her mother's example, young

Mary remained tolerant of those who followed the new Protestant doctrine.

While Mary was safe and pampered in France, her mother faced increasing difficulties in Scotland—the country remained in turmoil as noble families vied for power and the Protestant reformers grew more numerous and vocal. In 1550, two years after her daughter had departed, Marie de Guise planned a trip to France to ask King Henry II for more military assistance for Scotland, as well as to visit her daughter. When Mary received word that her mother was coming, she wrote a letter to her grandmother promising she would work hard at her studies and "become very wise, in order to satisfy her [mother's] understandable desire to find me as satisfactory as you and she could wish."

Once Marie arrived, she and her daughter traveled to Normandy where Henry II held a gala. They spent as much time together as they could, but after a year, Marie prepared to return to Scotland. Mary begged her to stay, but although she was tempted to remain in France, Marie knew that she had to return to Scotland to keep the Scottish Parliament from usurping her power. She renewed her vow to Mary that she would keep the Scottish crown safe for her, and then left. Mary never saw her mother again.

After her mother's departure, Mary resumed her privileged life in the French court. As she entered adolescence, however, she began to demand changes. At thirteen, she insisted on having her own estate and her own servants. The princesses Elizabeth and Claude had moved from the royal nursery to their mother's rooms at court, and Francis had been given his own household, leaving Mary without her childhood companions. If Mary were to have her own household, her mother would have to pay for it. Heavily in debt, Marie was reluctant, but Mary's uncles intervened on the young queen's behalf. If Mary was more independent of royal control, they would have greater influence over her. Their niece, said the cardinal, "already possessed of a high and noble spirit that lets her annoyance be very plainly seen if she is unworthily treated," wished to be grown up and "to exercise her independent authority." Under this pressure, Mary's mother agreed to finance the new household.

Although Mary had her own household, she still had a governess. After a scandal, her Scottish governess left France and was replaced by a Frenchwoman, Madame de Parois. Soon, however, the new governess wrote to Marie complaining about Mary's indulgent lifestyle and asking Marie for more money. Mary complained that Madame de Parois had criticized her for giving away expensive gowns to her aunts. Her governess was angry that Mary had not given the gowns to her, remarking, "I see that you're afraid in case you enrich me! Obviously you mean to keep me poor."

Mary wrote emotional letters to her mother, claiming that the troubles with her governess were making her sick and that the woman had almost brought on her death: "Because I was afraid of falling under your displeasure, and because I grieved at hearing through these false reports so many disputes and so much harm said of me." Soon, Madame de Parois resigned her position.

Mary fell ill during the conflict with her governess. One of the English ambassadors in Scotland later reported, "I hear she is troubled with such sudden passions after any great unkindness or grief of mind." Mary suffered bouts of severe stomach pain that lasted from a few days to several weeks, usually during times of stress, a condition that remained with her for her entire life.

Mary's uncle, Charles de Guise, Cardinal of Lorraine, stood out as the most prominent politician at Henry's court. He traveled with the royal household and acted as Mary's mentor, advising her about etiquette and politics. Her other uncle, Francis, Duke of Guise, was a brilliant military commander who, when not away fighting, often invited Mary to visit his château. After Mary acquired her own household, the duke and the cardinal became more involved in her life.

Mary's uncle, Francis, Duke of Guise

They wanted to keep the ear of the future queen of France, and guide her pursuit of the English throne.

Her uncles encouraged her to take an interest in Scottish affairs. The ineffective Arran had finally given up the role of regent, in exchange for a French dukedom, and Marie de Guise had been appointed in his place. At her uncles' urging, Mary sent her mother blank pieces of paper signed with her name, so that Marie de Guise could use her daughter's signature for official business. As Mary spent time with her uncles, she grew to admire their strong bond and loyalty to her and her mother. Later, in Scotland, when she expected this same familial loyalty from her Stewart relatives, she would be disappointed.

In the spring of 1558, when Mary was fifteen and Francis fourteen, King Henry declared it was time for them to marry. Henry was eager to strengthen relations with Scotland so he could call on Scottish forces to fight against England.

Just before the wedding, Mary signed a secret treaty with Henry II that placed Scotland under French control if Mary died childless. Her willingness to sign such a treaty attested to her trust in Henry and her uncles. It also revealed a trait that would bring her much grief as an adult—a reluctance to oppose the wishes of men she loved and admired.

3

Line of Succession

Mary's royal wedding was held on Sunday, April 24, 1558. King Henry II was determined to create a dazzling pageant, despite the fact that France was deep in debt. Fifes and tambourines heralded the arrival of the Swiss Guards, who led the procession into Notre Dame Cathedral in the center of Paris. First the Duke of Guise, followed by musicians, the king's gentlemen-in-waiting, churchmen, and Henry's relatives solemnly walked down the long aisle. Next came several magnificently costumed cardinals, Mary's uncle Charles among them. Then the groom passed through the massive doors of the cathedral, flanked by two younger brothers.

Francis was scarcely inside the church before all eyes diverted from him to his bride. Mary Stuart astonished the

Contemporary photo of the Notre Dame Cathedral where Mary and Francis II were married on April 24, 1558.

guests by dressing in white, the traditional color of mourning in sixteenth-century France and unheard of for a joyous occasion. Mary had disregarded custom and chosen white because it flattered her pale complexion and set off the russet shine of her hair, which fell loosely over her shoulders in another defiance of tradition. She wore a diamond pendant, a gift from Henry II, around her neck and her gold crown glittered with sapphires, emeralds, diamonds, rubies, and pearls. Mary's beauty was luminous and her stature regal. Only one thing detracted from the joyful day, the absence of her mother, who did not think it was prudent to leave Scotland to share in her daughter's wedding.

Mary basked in the attention, well aware of her impact. Much had already been written about her elegant height, the delicate bones, fragile complexion, the warm amber of her hair and eyes, and the heavy eyelids that gave her a sensual look. She was often compared to her father, who had also possessed a strong, sensual appeal. Most of her contemporaries believed that Mary was the most beautiful princess in Europe, and her charm and charisma added to her beauty.

After their marriage, Mary and Francis grew closer, even though their differences became more obvious with every passing year. Francis shared little of Mary's interests in the arts or court affairs, preferring to hunt and play tennis. He possessed none of Mary's vivaciousness. Furthermore, ill health continued to plague him. He was slow to reach puberty—in all likelihood, the young couple never consummated their marriage. Regardless, Mary had a deep affection for him. Francis had been her childhood playmate, and as husband and wife, they continued to spend a great deal of time together, walking in the gardens, and hunting with their favorite horses.

Many things did trouble Mary, though. She worried constantly about her absent mother, especially in regards to the political and religious turmoil in Scotland. She was also concerned about her own health. She had not outgrown the bouts of illness she had suffered as a child and suffered sudden spells that left her in pain, dizzy, and short of breath.

In November of 1558, the English queen Mary Tudor, who had tried to restore Catholicism as the state religion in England, died childless. The question of English succession was complicated and controversial. Mary Tudor had been the daughter of Henry VIII and Catherine of Aragon. As noted, Henry VIII had divorced Catherine to wed Anne Boleyn and in the process broke the English Church away from Rome. Henry VIII hoped his new wife would produce a male heir to the English throne, but they had only one surviving child, a daughter named Elizabeth. Although Henry finally got his long-desired male heir from a later marriage, the son, Edward VII, had died childless, leaving Mary Tudor next in line.

Now Mary was dead and Elizabeth was Henry's last surviving child. The Catholic Church still did not recognize Henry's divorce, rendering Elizabeth illegitimate to the pope and the Catholics, and ineligible to inherit the throne. Henry II of France agreed with the pope that Elizabeth was illegitimate, meaning, in his interpretation, and that of many others in Europe, that his daughter-in-law, Mary Stuart, who was the great-granddaughter of Henry VII, was Mary Tudor's legitimate heir and the true English queen.

Making the claim that Mary should be the English queen was bold, but Henry II of France was not yet ready to enter into war to enforce the claim. The English Parliament acknowledged Elizabeth as the rightful heir and in January 1559 she was crowned queen of England and Ireland. Although he was not in a position to go to war, Henry II proclaimed that his daughter-in-law Mary Stuart was the rightful queen of Scotland, England, and Ireland. He even had Mary's banner emblazoned with England's royal arms to join the emblems of France and Scotland. Still, Henry II held back from trying to enforce Mary's claim, especially since the pope never acknowledged Elizabeth as the queen of England, and he also refused to name Mary Stuart as the rightful heir.

When Elizabeth Tudor was crowned queen of England in 1559, Henry II of France refused to accept her coronation. Instead he declared that Mary was queen. *(Courtesy of National Portrait Gallery, London)*

Mary's claim to the English throne, and her position in the line of succession, became one of the central issues of Mary's life. It placed her in a precarious situation because Queen Elizabeth could never rest completely as long as a rival claimant, who inevitably became a rallying point for resentful Catholics, was alive. Mary remained focused on her claim to the English throne and was fascinated by her cousin Queen Elizabeth.

Less than a year after Elizabeth became the English queen, tragedy propelled Mary onto the French throne. During the festivities celebrating his daughter's betrothal to Philip II of Spain, a marriage designed to create an alliance between two Catholic kingdoms, Henry II arranged a three-day jousting tournament. On the last day of the competition, the king insisted on taking one last challenge. Queen Catherine begged him not to joust again—she had dreamed that he would be pierced in one eye by a lance and die—but Henry insisted. During the joust, Henry's opponent's lance split in two; one fragment entered Henry's right eye, the second penetrated his throat. King Henry II died ten days later.

Francis, an immature boy, was suddenly the king of France, and Mary, already queen of Scotland, was now also queen of one of the most powerful countries in Europe. Francis was fifteen; she was a year and a half older.

Neither Francis nor Mary had experience ruling. The Guise uncles moved into their long-desired position as principal advisors on affairs of state. This was the moment Mary's uncles had long anticipated.

Francis preferred hunting and other recreational activities to dealing with matters of government. He did not fit the model of the brave, warrior king that was the ideal of the era. He openly feared for his personal safety, and Mary was often called upon to try to alleviate his anxiety about assassination or kidnapping.

Francis had good cause to be nervous. In March of 1560, while the king and the court were at the castle of Amboise, his counselors uncovered a plot to kidnap him. The conspirators were French Protestants who wanted to remove the king from the Catholic influence of the Guise brothers. The conspirators hoped to have the leader of the Bourbon family appointed as regent. The Bourbons were next in the line of succession after Francis' younger brothers and rivals to the ruling Valois family. Some prominent Bourbons had become Huguenots. The conspiracy was foiled, the conspirators captured and hanged in the streets of Amboise,

This anonymous engraving shows the execution of the Amboise conspirators on March 15, 1560. A crowd of more than 10,000 onlookers came to glimpse the carnage.

but the experience severely damaged Francis' confidence.

In Scotland, as in France, tensions were rising between Catholics and Protestants. The Protestant nobles turned to England for help in their scheme to remove Marie de Guise as regent and to reinstate the Protestant Earl of Arran (now the duke of Chatelherault.) In February 1560, Scotland, represented by the Lords of the Congregation—Scottish Protestants—signed the Treaty of Berwick with England. The treaty called for English troops to fight against Marie de Guise and her French forces. France was in debt after a long series of wars against the Austrians and Italians, and Francis could not afford to send more troops to help Marie. He asked her instead to negotiate with the Protestant nobles, and a second treaty, the Treaty of Edinburgh, was signed by the French and the Scots. This document called on both the French and English armies to leave Scotland and for Francis and Mary to recognize Elizabeth as the queen of England.

Shortly after the negotiations ended, the Scottish Parliament, acting without the consent of Marie de Guise, announced Scotland's break from the Catholic Church. Mary remained Catholic, though the official religion of her home country and kingdom was now Protestant. The Scottish Parliament also passed a law forbidding anyone to celebrate Catholic Mass; a third conviction for celebrating Mass would result in a death sentence.

On June 11, 1560, Marie de Guise died at the age of forty-four. Her death was not mourned in most quarters of Scotland. The people had never fully accepted her, and they resented her inviting the French army to their shores. When her uncle Charles told her that her mother had died, Mary collapsed with grief.

After her mother's death, Mary began paying close attention to Scottish politics. She criticized the Scottish nobles, saying, "My subjects in Scotland do their duty in nothing, nor have they performed their part in one thing that belongeth to them. I am their Queen and so they call me, but they use me not so." She also refused to ratify the Treaty of Edinburgh, which called on her to give up her claim to the English throne. Mary's words to the British ambassador in announcing her refusal to sign contained a warning to Queen Elizabeth: "The Queen my good sister may be assured to have a better neighbor of me being her cousin, than of the rebels, and so I pray you signify."

Mary needed to have children to continue the dynasty. She wanted to become a mother, but it was not likely to happen with Francis. The king's poor health had long worried the Guises—should something happen to the young king, they could lose their influence over the French crown.

Then, in November of 1560, while on a hunting trip, the king began to complain of an earache. The next day he fainted at Mass and was taken to his chamber, where Mary and his mother Catherine kept constant watch over him. He was clearly dying. Still grieving over her mother, Mary prepared to say good-bye to her childhood companion and husband. She nursed him and comforted him, refusing to leave his side, but there was nothing to be done. Inflammation had spread to his brain. After only seventeen months on the throne, Francis II of France died, and Mary donned a white robe and entered a darkened room for forty days of mourning.

Mary Queen of Scots in a white mourning veil and hood after losing her husband, father-in-law, and mother. *(Courtesy of National Galleries of Scotland)*

4

Adieu, France!

Mary Stuart emerged from her mourning a changed woman. In a few months she had become queen of France, lost her beloved mother, and been widowed. She was not yet twenty years old. The stress and emotional blows were devastating, but she had no choice but to face her future with as much energy and practicality as she could muster. Whatever her private grief or anxiety about her fate, she presented an outward face of optimism and self-control.

Mary's uncles and other advisors searched for a suitable new husband. The Guises needed her to be placed in a new position of power, and Mary was in agreement. She had been a queen since she was six days old and had been betrothed to the future king of France as a small child. She could imagine no less status for herself.

The most obvious choice for a new husband was her brother-in-law Charles, the next in line to the French throne. Immediately after Francis' death, Catherine de' Medici had arranged for ten-year-old Charles to be named as Francis' successor and to have herself named regent until he came of age. The biggest obstacle to the marriage, ironically, was the Guise uncles who wanted it to come to pass so desperately. Catherine wanted her own wealthy Italian family to dominate the French court and in order for that to happen, the Guise influence needed to be diminished.

Mary knew the chances of Catherine agreeing to the arrangement were slim and began pursuing an alliance with Don Carlos, heir to the Spanish throne. Don Carlos was the son of King Philip's first wife, and the stepson of Mary's sister-in-law, Catherine's daughter Elizabeth. Don Carlos was Mary's inferior in terms of looks and intelligence, but she understood the practical advantage of a marriage to him.

Negotiations proceeded slowly because of the secret opposition of Catherine, who did not want Mary to overshadow her daughter at the Spanish court. While promising Mary that she was working to arrange the marriage, Catherine wrote secretly to Elizabeth, urging her to persuade King Philip not to allow it.

As the negotiations dragged on, Mary took steps to guide her future. Although mindful of how her mother had struggled to protect her birthright in Scotland, Mary was reluctant to return. Since her mother's death, the country had been ruled by a group of Protestant nobles, the Lords of the Congregation, one of whom was Mary's half-brother and childhood

Mary attempted to arrange a marriage with Don Carlos, who was in line to become king of Spain.

idol, James Stewart. These powerful nobles preferred that she remain in France. Mary was Catholic and, in their eyes, a foreigner. Undeterred, Mary wrote a letter informing them that she was willing to return to Scotland and take her place as its rightful ruler.

Mary maintained independence in her dealings with Queen Elizabeth and Elizabeth's Secretary of State, William Cecil. The Treaty of Edinburgh, which provided for withdrawal of both French and British troops from Scotland, had never been ratified, although most terms of the treaty had been met. Remaining unfinished was action on the clause requiring

Mary's half-brother, James Stewart, resented his sister's higher ranking.

Mary to renounce her claim to the throne of England. When Elizabeth had sent Mary her condolences on Francis' death she had also asked her to ratify the Treaty. Mary responded that she was unwilling to renounce her claim until she had conferred with her advisors in Scotland.

Elizabeth saw this for what it was—a stalling tactic. Mary had no intention of giving up her claim to the English throne. Not only did her Catholic supporters insist she was the true queen, but if Elizabeth died childless, Mary was indisputably next in line. Cecil, Elizabeth's Secretary of State, regarded Mary's refusal to ratify the Treaty as a treasonous act because it refused to recognize Elizabeth as the rightful ruler of England. He was convinced that Mary was forming a Catholic conspiracy to depose his queen. Over the next two decades, Cecil continued to see Mary as a threat to Elizabeth, and he did everything he could to curtail her power. In the end, Cecil would play a part in Mary's death.

In 1564 it became clear that the marriage to Don Carlos would not materialize when Catherine revealed her hand and offered her daughter, Marguerite, as a possible bride for the Spanish heir. At the same time, Mary had some encouraging news from Scotland. It seemed that she would be welcomed if she returned as queen. She had held two meetings with Scottish emissaries. The first was with a representative from the Catholic Church, who assured her 20,000 troops were in the north and ready to support Mary if she openly opposed James Stewart and the Lords of the Congregation and wanted to fight to restore Catholicism as the official Scottish religion. Much of the northern highlands had remained Catholic, being geographically far removed from the reform movement. Mary refused the offer, but she was heartened to learn of such a large number of devoted followers.

James Stewart also came to France and met with Mary. During the meeting Mary offered James a prestigious post if he would revert to Catholicism. He refused and asked her to give up her Catholic faith. She refused. They did reach other compromises, however. James told Mary that if she would acknowledge Protestantism as the official state church, she would be allowed to practice her faith in private, even attending daily Mass held in secret. Mary agreed. She considered this concession to be a prudent decision and indicated her willingness to be tolerant of other religions, though devout in her own, and her ability to make a distinction between personal faith and public policy. This was not a trait shared by many European rulers.

Mary came away from the meeting convinced James could be a trusted advisor, but James was only concerned with his own ambitions. Now thirty, twelve years older than his royal half-sister, James was deeply resentful that Mary, and not he, had succeeded James V. To this end he cultivated a relationship with England and Queen Elizabeth. Soon after his meeting with Mary, he reported on their conversation to the English ambassador, who in turn reported to Elizabeth.

Once James was back in Scotland, the Lords of the Congregation discussed the practicality of inviting Mary back as their queen. They determined that her return suited their needs—while they would have most of the power, Mary would please the people.

While Mary was deciding her future, two men who would play important roles in that future visited the French court. One was Henry Stuart, Lord Darnley, a pretty lad of sixteen whose mother hoped Mary would consider for a husband. Darnley was a cousin of Mary's and a descendant of the royal houses of both England and Scotland, meaning he and his family harbored their own royal ambitions. The other visitor was James Hepburn, Earl of Bothwell, who had visited Mary while Francis was alive. During his visit, Bothwell assured Mary of his loyalty to her and reminded her that he had supported Marie de Guise during her regency. Both men were Mary's future husbands.

On June 10, 1564, Mary received a letter from James Stewart asking her to return to Scotland. Mary then wrote to Queen Elizabeth asking for a passport for safe passage. England controlled the seas between France and Scotland, and it would be in Elizabeth's interest to seize Mary before she returned to Scotland, where she could pose a threat. But Elizabeth, angry at Mary's refusal to sign the Treaty of Edinburgh, refused to grant the request.

In responding to Elizabeth's refusal to grant safe passage, Mary wisely took the high road. She wrote confidently that she would reach her country safely, protected by her own people, and reminisced that she had journeyed safely through those same waters thirteen years ago in spite of Elizabeth's father's efforts to abduct her. She then reiterated her intention to consult with her official advisors before deciding if she would sign the Treaty of Edinburgh.

Mary departed from Calais with a fleet of galley ships under the admiralty of Bothwell. She had no guarantee of safe passage as she returned to a land she knew was in turmoil. The four Marys returned with her. It had been a sunny August day that welcomed Mary to France thirteen years ago; she left France on another August day, this one

Despite Queen Elizabeth's refusal to guarantee Mary a safe journey home to Scotland, she embarked on the trip anyway. *(Courtesy of The Bridgeman Art Library)*

gray and misty. Distraught at leaving the land she had come to call home, she stood at the bow muttering, "Adieu, France! Adieu, France! Adieu donc, ma chère France . . . Je pense ne vous revoir jamais plus." [Goodbye, France! Goodbye, France! Goodbye now, my dear France . . . I do not think I shall ever see you again.]

It took five days for Mary to cross from her old to her new life. When she disembarked in Scotland she was, as the Catholic emissary had promised, welcomed with a joyous celebration. The greetings were wild and unrestrained; huge bonfires blazed and crowds cheered Mary along her progression to Holyrood Palace in Edinburgh. She had retained her knowledge of Scots and spoke to the people in their own language.

When she arrived at the palace, Mary was shown to her apartments in the northwest tower. Under her palace window hundreds gathered to serenade her. Holyrood was situated on the edge of the capital city of Edinburgh, close to the hub of activity, yet near the wild country. After only a few days it became obvious that the atmosphere at the Scottish court was much more solemn than the French court. There was less frivolity, music, and dancing. Instead, an attitude of extreme seriousness prevailed.

Over the next months the people often saw their queen out riding through the countryside, hunting and hawking. She became a romantic figure, enhanced by her exquisite taste in dress. The Scottish people seemed proud to have such a young and beautiful example in Mary.

But for all the Scots that admired Mary, she did have an

Mary returned to joyous greetings at Holyrood Palace in Edinburgh. *(Courtesy of The Bridgeman Art Library)*

ardent enemy. Protestant leader John Knox was a committed Calvinist and intolerant of the Catholic religion. Over the years he had repeatedly urged the use of violence to stamp out Catholicism and had supported the killing of any ruler he considered unacceptable. He also believed that women were inferior to men and quoted biblical passages to support his belief that no woman should ever rule over a man.

John Calvin

Martin Luther (1483-1546) sparked the great schism in Western Christianity that came to be called the Protestant Reformation when he nailed a list of ninety-five complaints on a church door in the German town of Wittenberg in 1517. The schism did not stop with Luther, however. Soon Protestantism itself began to splinter into competing beliefs. The most significant of the new Protestant faiths that diverted from Luther's original doctrine was led by the Frenchman John Calvin (1509-1564).

Calvin's father was a lawyer who worked to reform the Catholic Church. Calvin also trained in the law and followed in his father's footsteps. Then, in 1530, King Francis I began arresting advocates of Catholic reform at the pope's request and Calvin fled France. He wandered Europe for a few years, during which he became a committed Protestant. When he settled down in Geneva, Switzerland in 1536, he had a reputation as a theologian and writer. Geneva had recently overthrown its Catholic rulers, and Calvin was invited to the city to set up a Protestant government. This is where Calvinism was born.

Although Calvin agreed with the basic tenet of Lutheranism—that salvation came from God's grace alone, not by good works or the intercession of saints—his doctrine of predestination was a new departure. Calvin spent years elaborating on what he meant by predestination, and it is highly complicated. Generally, while Luther believed it was possible for all believers to experience God's saving grace, Calvin argued that because God was all-knowing and all-powerful, those destined to be saved, the so-called elect, were saved at birth, and those condemned were powerless to alter their fate. Furthermore, the elect were God's instruments with a duty to see to it that God's laws were obeyed. This eventually led to the attempted imposing and maintaining of the Calvinistic interpretation of God's laws throughout Europe and North America, particularly in New England.

Calvinism spread clandestinely throughout Europe, and Geneva was visited by thousands of converts. John Knox, the founder of the Calvinist Scottish Presbyterian Church, first visited Geneva in 1554 and returned frequently to consult with Calvin until 1559, when he returned to Scotland.

When Mary tried to celebrate Mass the first Sunday after her arrival, Protestants interrupted the service and attacked a servant carrying articles used in the Mass. To lessen tensions, and to squelch the rumors, many of them fostered by Knox, that she was determined to return Scotland to Catholicism, Mary issued a proclamation promising that no one would interfere with the existing state of religion in Scotland. She made it clear that death would be the punishment for anyone who attempted to overthrow the status quo.

In response, John Knox preached a fiery attack on the Mass. Aware of the potential danger of Knox, Mary demanded a meeting with him. She explained, with poise and assurance, that she had no wish to interfere with the religious settlement or to stop Protestants from practicing their faith. She also made it clear that she separated her own religious beliefs from her role as queen. It was the peace of Scotland that was of utmost importance and she would not allow religious differences to jeopardize it. She began to weep, making Knox look like a rude bully. He finally agreed to tolerate Mary for the time being, but he continued to assert his right to rise up against any ruler who opposed God's will—as he interpreted it.

Knox continued to be Mary's fiercest critic. He denounced her religious practices as devilish and had no respect for her classical education, her extensive library, and her love of music and poetry. He particularly disapproved of her dancing, denouncing it from the pulpit as not something an honest, respectful woman would do.

For Mary, who had been brought up in the more socially liberated French court, dancing was an expression of her pleasure in life. She also liked to dress up and adopted the custom of wearing the so-called "highland mantles"—loose cloaks reaching to the ground that were usually embroidered. Queen Mary had three such mantles—one white, one blue and one black—embroidered in gold. Mary also loved dressing up in male clothes and wandering the streets incognito, mingling with her subjects. A writer of the time commented, "Only a lady of perfect beauty with perfect legs should attempt such a disguise, in order that no man should be able to tell to which sex she really belonged, whether she was a handsome boy or the beautiful woman she was in reality."

Knox tried to scandalize these youthful pursuits, but Mary's actions were typical of royal escapades and entertainments. During her first years in Scotland, Mary was a beautiful and unattached girl who could have indulged in anything she wanted, but her behavior was above reproach.

Somewhere between the adoration of the Scottish people and the hatred of Protestants like John Knox, there was the complex relationship between Mary and the Scottish nobility. Scotland was still more of a medieval feudal society than a Renaissance monarchy, in that the nobles behaved largely autonomously. For the most part, the Scottish nobles were rough, uneducated, and violent. Many of the noble leaders were scarcely older than Mary—young men who had inherited their land and titles when their fathers had been killed in the battle of Solway Moss.

The Scottish nobility had land but little money, often making them susceptible to corruption. They were notoriously unstable, with rapidly shifting loyalties that were determined more by personal advantage than any code of ethics or patriotism, and they had a propensity to settle most conflicts with violence—even cold-blooded murder.

Although the nobility in France were equally ambitious and capable of great cruelty, their misdeeds were cloaked in civilized behavior. Mary, accustomed to these men of education and civility, was not prepared to deal with the brutish Scottish nobility. She often turned to the advice of others, and as her trust of James Stewart indicated, often was unable to discern who had her best interests at heart.

Mary had to select a Privy Council made up of members of the nobility, six of whom were to be in constant attendance on her to dispatch daily business. The Privy Council sat in the royal palace and was vested with executive powers.

The role of Parliament was more remote. It assembled to vote approval or disapproval of acts presented to it by the Lords of the Articles, a committee that communicated between the queen and Parliament. The Lords of the Articles, in turn, tended to support whatever faction controlled the Privy Council.

The Scottish crown had widespread powers, but the problem was implementing these powers. In addition to being somewhat at the mercy of the nobles, the crown had two other weaknesses: no standing army and no money to raise one. If Mary wanted to wage war, she would have to appeal to the nobility to support her and to lead men personally loyal to them into battle.

Mary called on her half-brother, James Stewart, to help her in her dealings with George, Earl of Huntly. Huntly controlled a string of family alliances in the Highlands of the northeast of Scotland and had a reputation for untrustworthiness in matters that did not directly affect his immediate clan. He was also a dedicated Catholic who was angry that Mary was not more aggressive on the part of Scottish Catholics.

The immediate situation Mary had to deal with, so soon after assuming the throne, involved Huntly's third son, John Gordon, who had been imprisoned for wounding a man in a street brawl but had escaped to his father's lands in the north. Mary was determined to show that the powerful Gordon family was not above the law. She was also infuriated that Gordon had publicly claimed Mary wanted to marry him.

Mary sought her half brother's approval to take an army north. James readily agreed; he had his own reasons for going against Huntly. The queen had recently granted James the earldom of Moray, from which Huntly had been profiting for years, and James wanted to publicly lay claim to the earldom himself. After an extended series of attacks and counterattacks, Huntly was killed on the battlefield and his son John was taken prisoner and sentenced to death. A second son, George

Gordon, was imprisoned. Mary would later release him, and he would become one of her most loyal supporters.

James insisted that Mary attend the execution of John Gordon in order to silence the rumors that she had sought to marry him. It was a terrible experience. She became ill at the sight of the bloody dismembering and could not leave her bed for days afterward.

James benefited the most from Huntly's demise. As Earl of Moray, he now controlled substantial lands in the north, further weakening the Catholic cause. However, defeating Huntly proved that Mary was committed to stopping any Catholic uprisings, helping her relations with the Protestants, at least temporarily.

Even as she was busy establishing herself as queen of Scotland, Mary continued to pursue her claim to the English throne. Shortly after arriving in Scotland she learned that Queen Elizabeth had finally sent the safe passage guarantee for her crossing. Mary followed up this gesture of goodwill by sending an envoy to Elizabeth to discuss succession. Mary was willing to give up her present claim to the English throne in return for Elizabeth's acknowledgment that she stood next in line if Elizabeth was not succeeded by a lawful child. In the negotiations, Elizabeth agreed that Mary was the one she would choose as her successor, but refused to make a formal acknowledgment. She claimed such a promise would make it impossible for her to have a relationship with Mary, pointing out that she could not possibly embrace the person who would constantly be a reminder of what was to happen after her death. Elizabeth also worried that the English people, being notoriously fickle, could easily find fault with Elizabeth and "have their eyes fixed upon that person that is next to succeed."

Mary was not popular in England, being Catholic and, in many people's eyes, French. Mary knew her best chance of assuring the succession was to have Elizabeth openly support her. Mary put all her energies into arranging a meeting with the English queen, confident that her charm could win Elizabeth's support. Mary wrote letters, sent verses and gifts, and even joked with the English ambassador about her fascination with her cousin. The English ambassador commented that, "This Queen wished that one of the two were a man, to make an end of all debates."

Elizabeth eventually agreed to the meeting. But it was called off because of an outbreak of religious civil war in France. Elizabeth said that it was not safe for her to travel to the north of England—the meeting was to take place on the border of England and Scotland—with war raging just across the English Channel. Moreover, Elizabeth could not appear to support the Catholic cause by meeting with Mary. Mary was devastated. Her hopes of establishing a personal relationship with Elizabeth, nurtured over the past two years, were lost.

The religious conflict in France took a more personal toll when her uncle, Duke Francis of Guise, whom Mary had loved as a father, was killed. At home, her lifelong friend Mary Fleming left the royal court to get married. It seemed that Mary was losing the people she cared about. She needed someone besides James Stewart to help her face the challenges of ruling a country. The French ambassador reported, "She has begun to marry off her Marys, and says that she wishes she herself were of that band."

5

Love and Murder

I n April of 1565, Mary changed, seemingly overnight, from a cautious, politically astute queen into an impetuous, passionate woman. She seemed no longer interested in listening to her advisors, or to even care about the opinion of Queen Elizabeth, whose approval had been her utmost concern for over two years. The only person who mattered was Henry Stuart, Lord Darnley.

Darnley had been suggested as a possible husband for Mary from time to time. He was Mary's step-second cousin and, like her, claimed a right of succession to the English throne. His family was Catholic, though he was not devout. His mother, the ambitious Countess of Lennox, had even sent him to France with the supposed purpose of offering condolences to

Mary was attracted to Henry Stuart, Lord Darnley, who stood tall and handsome. *(Courtesy of National Galleries of Scotland)*

Mary after the death of Francis, but actually to present him to the young queen as a marriage prospect.

Mary had not taken particular interest in young Darnley when he came to France. She was focused on arranging a marriage with Don Carlos of Spain, a political maneuver, governed by her head, not her heart. In the ensuing years she had not been without help in the husband search. Much of Europe, caught up in the religious wars, was anxious to find Mary a second husband—a strategically arranged marriage could unite various powers, and bring about some stability. But the search for a proper husband for the queen was not an easy one—every decision was fraught with political importance, and eventually the search lagged.

Into this impasse, in March of 1565, stepped Lord Darnley. The young lord and his father, the Earl of Lennox, had been in England and wanted to return home to Scotland. Elizabeth asked Mary to reinstate Lennox's lands, lost during the regency of Mary's mother, and Lennox and his son visited Mary when they returned to Scotland.

This time Mary took notice of the dashing young Darnley. He stood more than six feet tall, pleasing Mary, who was tall for a woman of her era. She remarked that, "He was the properest and best proportioned long man that ever she had seen." Darnley also had a head of blond hair, a short nose, hazel eyes, full lips, and an oval chin.

Mary and Darnley spent a month getting to know each other, but little passion was generated between them initially. Even when news came that Philip of Spain had declared his son Don Carlos to be insane, and therefore unsuitable for marriage, Mary made no move to encourage Darnley.

Then, in April, Darnley caught a cold that turned into measles and confined him to his bed. Mary threw herself into nursing him and was constantly by his side. As she tended to his health, she fell in love with him. Suddenly, it seemed that all of her unfulfilled physical desire was directed at this handsome youth. She was determined to marry Darnley as soon as possible.

Mary's choice of husband shocked those close to her. They could see that her passion for Darnley had blinded her to his faults—faults that were wholly apparent to everyone else.

Darnley was spoiled and arrogant, lacking in judgment, and viewed everyone and everything through his own selfish lens. But all attempts to caution Mary were wasted. The English ambassador, who had grown to admire Mary, wrote in despair of the "poor Queen whom ever before I esteemed so worthy, so wise, so honourable in all her doing" who was now so changed by love.

Elizabeth was worried by Mary's decision to marry Darnley. She saw it as an attempt to combine Darnley's claim to the English succession with Mary's and feared that they would put forth an immediate claim to her throne. She also opposed

Much to the disapproval of those around her, Mary wed Lord Darnley in 1565.

the marriage because of concerns that Darnley's Catholicism would tip the balance and tie Scotland more tightly to Catholicism and the Pope. Elizabeth's opposition to the marriage soon fueled opposition in Scotland, particularly from Protestant quarters.

Many nobles disliked Darnley because of old feudal and familial conflicts. James Stewart was particularly concerned that the influence he had over Mary would be lost. He withdrew from court in protest of the wedding and began to foment a rebellion.

Mary, who previously had been sensitive to political ramifications during her hunt for a new spouse, turned a deaf ear to all the opposition. Nothing could deter her from marrying Darnley, and before long, she got her wish.

At her second wedding, she wore a black dress and hood, symbolizing that she was a widow and dowager queen of France. During the feasting and dancing following the marriage ceremony she changed out of her mourning dress. The next day she ordered the heralds to declare Darnley to be King Henry of Scotland, alienating many Scottish lords because this title had not been approved by the Privy Council.

Mary's declaration did not grant Darnley the "crown matrimonial,"—that would have given him the right to rule on his own if she died, and would allow him to pass on the crown through his bloodline, although Darnley and his family wanted her to do so. But this could be conferred only by the members of Parliament, who were in no mood to grant even more power to Darnley, even if Mary had requested it. Mary's declaration, however, made clear her esteem for her new husband. She advanced his power by announcing that all documents would be signed by them both, with her signature in the place of greater importance.

Meanwhile, James Stewart went to England, where he asked Queen Elizabeth to help fund his plot against Mary on the grounds that the marriage to Darnley had undermined the Protestant cause. Mary, insisting that her marriage was not a religious issue, retaliated by asking the Scottish Parliament to seize her half-brother's lands, as well as those of any nobles who supported him.

Mary soon learned that James was planning to abduct Darnley and his father and take them to England. In an attempt to resolve the issue she offered safe-conduct to James and his followers if they would appear before her and explain their actions. James refused, allowing Mary to brand him a traitor. His properties were seized, and eight days later, Mary announced her intention to take arms against the rebels.

Having no standing army, Mary gathered soldiers by pledging her jewels for payment. On August 26, she rode out of Edinburgh, with Darnley at her side. They pursued the rebels, but James fled to London.

The Chaseabout Raid, as James' rebellion came to be known, altered how Mary governed the country. During her first four years in Scotland, she had not been able to come to terms with the shifting allegiances of the nobility. She had tried to honor her commitments, but after James' treason she realized she could not trust the nobles. She created a new staff—one that was not manned by powerful nobles—to handle her affairs with France, with the Pope, and with Spain. This infuriated the Scottish nobility and set off a chain of events that changed the course of Mary's life.

Amongst the new political servants was an Italian Catholic named David Riccio, who had come to Scotland four years before with the Italian ambassador. Riccio was considered a physically ugly man, of short stature and hunched posture. Still, Mary liked and trusted him. His first position in her entourage was as secretary in charge of French correspondence, but he soon was always near at hand to advise or comfort her when she faced difficult decisions. Before long he was insisting that all matters for the queen's attention first pass through him, further infuriating the nobles.

As Riccio gained favor, Darnley was quickly falling from the pedestal he'd been placed upon by Mary. The new king was undisciplined and had little interest in the day-to-day operations of government, preferring to spend his time riding and hunting. But, while he didn't like the work of ruling, he

John Knox scolds the women of the court of Mary Queen of Scots. *(Library of Congress)*

reveled in the power and privilege of his position and lusted after more. He hounded Mary to ask Parliament to confer on him the crown matrimonial.

Mary realized Darnley was not the strong, supportive figure she wanted by her side. He drank excessively, and was moody, vain, and jealous. She began to hear rumors of his prowling the city streets at night, engaging in illicit conduct. She became pregnant early in the marriage, but Darnley soon spoiled her happiness by insinuating that Riccio, whom Darnley had come to see as a bitter rival, was the father.

Mary's unborn baby gave her another serious claim to the English throne at a time when her hold on the Scottish crown was under siege. James Stewart was back in England, trying again to finance an invasion. Closer to home, her marriage to Darnley had incited John Knox to intensify his verbal assaults on her. He gave sermons on the evil of Catholic marriage and made claims of having knowledge of plots, directed from Rome, to restore Catholicism to Scotland, despite Mary's often repeated promises to not attempt to alter the state religion.

There was a more pressing threat growing in Mary's own home. As the rift between Mary and Darnley widened, he became receptive to rumors that Mary was having an affair with Riccio. Scottish nobles, infuriated at Riccio's influence, seized on the rift and began suggesting to Darnley that if the queen and her unborn baby, which they insinuated was probably not his, disappeared, it would leave the throne open for him to seize in his own right. Darnley, frustrated that Mary had not asked for him to be granted crown matrimonial rights, was intrigued by the scheme, although there was no evidence that Mary and Riccio were lovers.

In March 1566, Darnley signed his name to a document, called a bond, drawn up by conspirators. It was also signed by the outlawed James Stewart. The bond stated their intention to acquire the crown matrimonial for Darnley, to uphold the Protestant religion, and to pardon the exiles from the Chaseabout Raid, as well as other unspecified plans summarized in the ominous phrase, "So shall they not spare life or limb in setting forward all that may bend to the advancement of his (Darnley's) honour."

Mary, awaiting the birth of her child, was oblivious of the plot. The conspirators decided to strike on the night of March 9, when the queen would be holding an intimate supper party in the small dining chamber of her four-room apartment at Holyrood Castle. The party was attended by Riccio and four other confidantes, including the Earls of Bothwell and Huntly. They had just begun the meal when Darnley suddenly appeared from behind a raised tapestry. He had arrived through a private stairway that connected his apartments below to Mary's on the second floor. Mary had seen little of her husband recently, and she was shocked when he appeared during her party.

Darnley took a seat beside Mary. Riccio was seated at the other end of the table. Moments later, the tapestry was raised again and Lord Ruthven, an old and sick noble who was thought to have magic powers, appeared. Ruthven was wearing a cap of steel and had on armor under his cloak. He stood behind Darnley and addressed the Queen: "May it please your Majesty, to let yonder man Davie (Riccio) come forth of your presence, for he has been over-long here."

Mary, realizing they were there to murder Riccio and quite possibly her, demanded to know what offense he had

Riccio struggles as he is pulled away to his own death. *(Courtesy of National Galleries of Scotland)*

committed. Ruthven answered, "Great offense!" and then denounced Riccio for having stained the queen's honor. Mary turned angrily to Darnley and asked what part he played in this conspiracy. He made no reply, then grabbed her as Ruthven went on to criticize the queen for her favoritism toward Riccio and the banishment of the Protestant lords.

Riccio, fearing for his life, retreated to a window at the end of the small room. When Ruthven lunged toward him, Mary's attendants moved to protect Riccio. Ruthven backed them off, saying, "Lay not hands on me, for I will not be handled."

This was a signal. Five more conspirators rushed into the room, brandishing pistols and daggers. The table was knocked over, and a pistol was aimed at Mary's belly. Desperate, Riccio grabbed Mary's skirts, but his fingers were pried off, and he was dragged away while crying, "Justice, justice," and "save me, madam, save me."

Then, at the top of the stairs leading down to Darnley's quarters, Riccio was stabbed more than fifty times, and his body was thrown down the stairway. The conspirators had also hoped to kill Bothwell and Huntly, both supporters of the queen, but they had escaped by jumping out a back window.

Riccio's death cries, as well as the yells and screams of the servants, disturbed others at the palace. The city alarm bell sounded, and people began gathering outside the palace.

Darnley went to the window and spoke to the crowd. The conspirators, who would not let Mary address the crowd, appeared to be in complete control of the situation, but opportunity was already slipping out of their grip.

While Darnley spoke to the excited citizens of Edinburgh, Ruthven informed Mary that more rebels were on their way to join forces with the conspirators and that she was their prisoner. When he and Darnley left the room to tend to their business, Mary sent one of her servants to find Riccio. Hearing that he was dead, she quickly dried her eyes. "No more tears now; I will think upon revenge."

Mary began plotting her vengeance. The first step was to escape from her captors, whom she believed would imprison her at Stirling. But, in order to escape, she needed Darnley. She suppressed her loathing toward him for his part in the conspiracy, and the next morning, when he came to her chamber, Mary was calm and resolute. She convinced her weak-willed husband that the murderers were not to be trusted and would soon turn on him. When more conspirators arrived the next day, Mary, more confident now that she had Darnley on her side, promised them pardon.

When her half-brother James arrived, Mary, unaware of his role in the plot, threw herself into his arms. "Oh, my brother, if you had been here they would not have used me thus." She was disappointed, then furious, when James embarked on a lofty speech on the virtue of forgiveness, but was still ignorant of his role in the murder.

Mary pretended to feel labor pains in order to keep them from trying to move her. She had to find an escape route out of Holyrood. Eliciting the help of faithful servants and three of her loyal attendants, Mary waited until midnight, when she and Darnley made their way down the private staircase, still covered with Riccio's blood, through the back hallways and servants' quarters to the outside, where they were met by loyal soldiers with horses. Mary rode behind one of the men; Darnley was on his own horse. They traveled fast through the dark night and five hours later arrived at Dunbar Castle on the coast. Mary, six months pregnant, must have found the journey arduous.

With Mary free and regaining her power, the conspiracy collapsed. Only nine days after Riccio's murder, Mary reentered Edinburgh triumphantly at the head of a force of eight thousand men. Bothwell, Huntly, and other loyal nobles, flocked to her side and the conspirators fled when they learned of Darnley's defection.

James, however, remained in Edinburgh. He had not been implicated in Riccio's murder and the Queen did not know he had signed the conspirators' agreement. In an attempt to reconcile her kingdom, Mary pardoned James and the other rebels involved in the Chaseabout Raid. She needed their help in this new crisis. Unaware that traitors stood at her side, she focused on avenging the murder of Riccio.

6

The Death of a King

Soon after driving the conspirators out of Scotland, Mary was presented with proof of Darnley's involvement in the conspiracy to kill Riccio. The conspirators, furious at Darnley's betrayal, sent her the bond he had signed agreeing to the murder in exchange for their support in his claim to the crown. Mary was convinced that Darnley had wanted to harm her and her unborn child. She detested the man she had defied almost everyone to marry only eight months before, but she kept her feelings to herself. She wanted to maintain the facade of marriage until the time was right to move against Darnley. Worried about the safety of her unborn child, she decided revenge would have to wait.

Mary genuinely desired a reconciliation with the Scottish nobility. She did not want her baby born into a Scotland torn by conflict, as it had been when she was born. She brought together the most dangerous of the longstanding rivals, James Stewart, on the one hand, and Bothwell and Huntly on the other, and made them members of her Privy Council. Both sides were united by a desire to be rid of Darnley, but this was a fragile foundation for long-term peace. Soon, James and his supporters were angry because Mary seemed to listen more to Bothwell than to them.

Mary decided that Bothwell was trustworthy. He had supported Mary's mother and helped thwart attempts to overthrow her when she was regent, and he consistently supported Mary since her return to Scotland. He was powerful and wealthy, with lands and a castle in the north and his own soldiers who followed him without question. Mary admired Bothwell's inclination toward risk-taking and adventure, and she was drawn to his manly bearing and blunt, swarthy features.

Unfortunately, Bothwell had less desirable traits that Mary either did not see or was willing to overlook. Although he had been educated in France, he had little of the gentility she had grown accustomed to in the French court. Bothwell tended to choose the quick, usually violent, solution to conflict. Mary had banished him from court more than once for fighting, but always welcomed him back.

Mary was warned to be cautious with Bothwell but, as with Darnley, she did not heed the advice. Most considered Bothwell to be "high in his own conceit, proud, vicious and vainglorious above measure, one who would attempt anything out of ambition," but the attraction she felt for him clouded her judgment.

On June 19, 1566, twenty-three-year-old Mary gave birth to a son, thus fulfilling her responsibility as a queen in giving

Mary Stuart presenting her newborn son, James, Prince of Scotland and heir of Great Britain, to her husband, Lord Darnley, Titular King of Scotland. *(Courtesy of the Granger Collection)*

Scotland a male heir. She named the son James. Five hundred bonfires were lit in Edinburgh and the surrounding hills to celebrate his birth, and the sound of artillery firing from the castle reverberated in the countryside.

Mary, anxious to assure Darnley that he was the father and prove the child's legitimacy, announced to her husband in public, "Here I protest to God as I shall answer to him at the great day of Judgment, that this is your son and no other man's son."

Mary enjoyed motherhood. She had the baby sleep in her own room in order to watch over him at night. However, the birth of the heir was not received with joy everywhere. When Queen Elizabeth heard the news, she began to feel even more pressure to marry, or, at the very least, to declare a successor.

After her son's birth, Mary no longer felt it necessary to keep up the pretense of being a wife to Darnley. She was confident that she had the support of the Privy Council to reveal her contempt for her husband. She announced to Darnley that she could never forget his treachery and pressured others not to show the king any friendship or support. The lords were quick to comply. Darnley raged over his lowered status and began plotting ways to line up support for a new conspiracy. His new scheme was to make himself the Catholic King of Scotland, supported by a strong foreign Catholic power, overthrow Mary, and raise James as a Catholic ruler.

Meanwhile, Mary, convinced that Darnley and his powerful Lennox family wanted to kidnap the baby James, took the prince to the protection of the royal nursery at Stirling Castle, where she had been kept as a baby.

The strain of murder, conspiracy, and childbirth took a toll on Mary's health. In October 1566 she became so ill it was said few expected her to survive. After taking a sixty mile round-trip journey in one day on horseback to visit with Bothwell, who had been wounded in a border skirmish, she was seized by prolonged fits of vomiting—"more than sixty times"—followed by spells of unconsciousness. A brief recovery gave way to a more serious attack, during which "all her limbs were so contracted, her face was so distorted, her eyes closed, her mouth fast and her feet and arms stiff and cold." In an attempt to cure her, physicians bandaged her tightly from her ankles to her neck, poured wine down her throat and administered an enema. Miraculously, considering this rough treatment, Mary vomited blood and began to recover, but she remained in precarious health, as well as depression, for weeks.

In November, Bothwell and several other lords met with Mary at Craigmillar Castle, on the outskirts of Edinburgh. The lords wanted to remove Darnley from power. All claimed to be motivated by a desire to protect the queen, but there

Current view of Craigmillar Castle, where Bothwell and other lords met with Mary to plot the demise of her husband, Lord Darnley.

was personal ambition at stake, particularly in the case of Bothwell, who wanted to marry Mary and become king himself.

Mary wanted to be rid of her husband, yet was conflicted, and had not fully recovered from her illness. But Mary was not inclined to wait. The shock of Riccio's murder, the years of stress, and disgust at her husband had already broken her health and nearly killed her. Earlier in her reign she had been more willing to be patient and to suppress her needs and wants if she thought it was in the public duty. Now the lords were convincing her that her private desire, to rid herself of Darnley, and the public good, were one in the same.

The lords discussed trying to arrange for a divorce from Darnley, if she agreed to pardon the exiled conspirators for Riccio's murder and to allow them to return to Scotland. The queen agreed reluctantly, but insisted that any divorce not jeopardize the legitimacy of her son.

Divorce was granted by papal authorities when it could be shown that the couple's blood relationship was too close. Occasionally, an annulment of a marriage was granted on that same ground. However, Mary and the lords knew a divorce or annulment was not likely to be granted. When one of the nobles suggested there were other means of removing Darnley, Mary replied, "I will that ye do nothing whereto any spot may be laid to my honor or conscience." This sounds very much as if she were saying that if Darnley was murdered, she wanted to be able to say she was not part of the plot. This was as close as she came to explicitly agreeing to a murder plot. She went on to make it clear that she would like Darnley to be gone, but she also asked

By granting pardons to the Earl of Morton, along with others who were involved in the plot to kill Riccio, Mary helped the plot to kill Lord Darnley along.

the lords to "let the matter be in the state as it is." The most critical point, however, is that she did not order them not to kill her husband.

Mary moved the growing plot to kill Darnley forward, intentionally or not, by granting the promised pardons to the Earl of Morton and the other Riccio conspirators. These men, whom Mary had vowed never to pardon, were victims of Darnley's betrayal, and they were determined to destroy him. They now joined James Stewart, Huntly, Bothwell, and others planning to assassinate the king.

In December, Mary's son James was baptized at Stirling Castle. Mary, ever mindful of an opportunity to reconcile with her cousin, named Queen Elizabeth as James' godmother. Elizabeth, feeling new pressure to name a successor, suggested that the Treaty of Edinburgh be rewritten to secure the English throne for James. This opened up a new avenue of communication on the succession.

During the three-day baptismal celebration, the most spectacular and costly festivity that Scotland had ever seen, Darnley withdrew to his rooms, unable to suffer the public humiliation of his reduced status. Bothwell was given his place of honor and welcomed diplomats from all over Europe in the king's absence. Masques, banquets, and other entertainments were held, culminating in a dramatic show of fireworks. Mary's favorite valet, Bastian, created an especially elaborate masque for the queen and her newly anointed son.

Darnley soon left Stirling for Glasgow and the Lennox family home, where he hoped to find a way to recover his power and to punish his wife for humiliating him. His father supported his quest for revenge. Together they plotted to kidnap little James, declare him King of Scotland, imprison Mary, and proclaim Darnley as regent until the king came of age. Darnley's planning was interrupted, though, when he fell ill. His body was covered in oozing sores, possibly from syphilis. His face was so ravaged that the vain king covered it with a thin material to conceal the pustules.

Mary went to Darnley and convinced him to return to Edinburgh. She feared, with reason, that Darnley was plotting against her, and that both she and her son were in danger from him. If Darnley remained in Glasgow she could not keep an eye on him, and he would have his father to help him plot against her. By luring him back to Edinburgh, she set in motion the events that would lead to his death.

Darnley agreed to return to Edinburgh. However, he asserted that he would not go to Craigmillar Castle, where he would be constantly watched, and possibly harmed, by its proprietor, Sir Simon Preston, one of Mary's trusted allies. Neither would he go to Holyrood where baby James and others would be exposed to his disease. Instead, Darnley arranged to stay about a mile away from Holyrood at the house of a friend, James Balfour. What Darnley did not know was that Balfour had turned against him

Balfour's house was one of a small group of buildings, a church and two or three other houses, in a complex known as Kirk o'Field. The wall surrounding Kirk o'Field had one opening and a walkway that led through the orchards and into the yard of Balfour's house. The house itself was two stories high, and the king's bedchamber was on the second floor. The conspirators planned to blow the king up as he slept by filling the cellar of Balfour's house with explosives.

When Darnley arrived he was still suffering from the sores, and a bathtub was moved next to his bed for him to soak in. Mary traveled the short distance from Holyrood several times to visit her husband, occasionally even spending the night in the bedchamber directly below Darnley. When the queen went to Kirk o'Field, members of the Court accompanied her, and a party atmosphere pervaded the small house. Everyone feasted and played cards, even Darnley. By early February the king had almost completely recovered, and he made plans to return to Holyrood on February 10. Once there, he hoped to regain all rights as Mary's husband.

On Sunday, February 9, 1567, Mary attended the wedding of her valet Bastian in the afternoon, and promised to return from Kirk o'Field in the evening to see the wedding masque and to take part in the dancing. She went to visit her husband around seven in the evening. The atmosphere among the guests was as lively as usual. What the revelers did not know was that in the cellar below, conspirators, spurred on by Darnley's plan to leave the next day, worked furiously to finish preparing and setting the explosives, their movements muffled by the noise of merrymaking in the rooms above.

At around eleven that night, Mary was reminded that she had promised to attend Bastian's wedding masque. Bastian had honored the prince with an elaborate masque at his christening and Mary could not disappoint him by not attending. She had planned to return to Kirk o'Field but now decided not to make the trip back there after the festivities.

The masque was almost over when Mary arrived. When it ended, Bothwell accompanied her back to Holyrood, where he and another noble visited with her until after midnight. Mary later claimed not to know that Bothwell's next stop after leaving her was to supervise the lighting of the fuse that would blow up Kirk o'Field.

At two o'clock in the morning of February 10, the sky over Edinburgh was lit by an explosion. Mary saw it from the palace. Dogs started barking all over the city people rushed from their houses. Word spread that Lord Darnley was dead. He and a servant had been found—not at the site of the explosion, but in the garden next to the house. There were no burns or bruises on their bodies—they had been strangled. At the news of the death of her husband, the queen immediately gave orders for Lord Bothwell to investigate the assassination.

The conspirators had planned for the blast to kill Darnley and destroy any clues to the identities of the assassins, but

After the murder of Lord Darnley, rumors began circulating that Mary and Lord Bothwell were lovers. This 1903 drawing by A. S. Hartrick portrays Mary and Bothwell together.

This picture depicting the events surrounding the murder and funeral of Lord Darnley was drawn shortly after the murders.

Darnley had apparently woken up and, looking out his window, saw activity in the yard below. Well aware that explosions were a common means of assassination for the Scots, Darnley used a rope and chair to lower himself and his servant to the ground. The explosion had gone off as they ran from the burning house. But the other conspirators, led by Morton, had come in through the opening in the wall and captured them as they tried to flee, and strangled them.

Before dawn, accusations of murder ran rampant.

Bothwell was suspected of being the ring leader and, inevitably, rumors spread that Mary and Bothwell had been lovers and had planned the murder of the young king together.

There is one unanswered question: was Mary part of the plot to murder Darnley? While there is no evidence that she knew the plotters intended to kill Darnley, she had recently witnessed a plot to rid the kingdom of Riccio unfold and her advisor had been murdered almost before her eyes. While Bothwell and the others might have avoided stating their intention explicitly, it is clearly possible to believe that she knew what would ensue. However, she had been ill and was preoccupied with making sure her child survived to become king. It is possible she simply expressed a desire to be rid of Darnley and the conspirators took their own initiative from there. It remains impossible to know for certain what Mary's role was, but the assassination of her husband defined the course of Mary's future.

Most Changed Woman

I n the days immediately following Darnley's murder, Mary
was at a crucial juncture. The choices she made would
determine her own future as well as the future of her
country. The best course of action probably would have been
to assert her authority as sovereign and seek public vengeance
for the assassins. This would have been a cynical, even cruel
act—even if she was not part of the conspiracy, she certainly
had to know who was. But this type of duplicitous behavior
was more the rule than the exception in Scotland, and it would
have helped to establish her innocence. But, either because
she was incapable of turning on Bothwell and the others, or
because she was uncertain of how best to react, Mary did
the worst thing possible—nothing.

This is the only known likeness of James Hepburn, the Earl of Bothwell.

None of the Scottish lords advised her on what to do. James Stewart left the country, as did Morton and Huntly, two other conspirators. Only Bothwell stayed at her side, seemingly ready to protect her and help her rule but actually scheming to find a way to make her his wife and himself the king.

As the Scottish people waited for Mary to act against the murderers, they began to suspect that she had been part of the conspiracy. Even Queen Elizabeth wrote to Mary, trying to shame her into action: "People for the most part are saying that you will look through your fingers at this deed instead of avenging it, and that you don't care to take action against those who have done you this pleasure." Elizabeth's rebuke was harsh, but accurate. Yet, although Mary had often sought Elizabeth's advice, she chose to ignore her this time. Instead, she turned to Bothwell, discarding Elizabeth's counsel that Mary "not fear to touch even him whom you have nearest to you if he was involved," because it would have meant prosecuting Bothwell for the murder of her husband. Mary instead put him in charge of the government, in the process losing her reputation, and eventually, her country and her freedom.

Even before the official forty day mourning period for Darnley was over, Bothwell moved his own men into the palace, controlling it as though it were a fortress. No one could gain an audience with Mary without first going through Bothwell. He even separated her from Prince James, returning the baby to Stirling Castle.

Meanwhile, Mary was being pressured to have Bothwell tried for killing Darnley. Much of the pressure came from Darnley's powerful father, the Earl of Lennox. She finally gave in and ordered a trial, but on the day it began, Bothwell filled Edinburgh with his supporters. Lennox, afraid of confronting Bothwell's militia, could not enter the city to press his case, and Bothwell was acquitted.

The Privy Council grew furious at Bothwell's arrogance. He challenged anyone who doubted his innocence to come forward and face him personally, and he triumphantly rode beside the queen to Parliament. All the while, Bothwell was trying to arouse enough support to carry out his plan to marry Mary. Another bond was drawn up, called the Ainslie Tavern Bond because of where it was signed, pledging the support of a group of nobles to Bothwell.

Mary, although she took Bothwell into her confidence and allowed him to visit her during her mourning period, refused his proposal of marriage several times. She refused even after he showed her the Ainslie Tavern Bond. Mary trusted him, and was attracted to him, but was not ready to enter into another marriage so soon after her husband's murder.

Bothwell would have been wise to bide his time. Instead, he responded to Mary's hesitancy by making it impossible for her not to marry him. Toward the end of April, Mary was at Stirling visiting her son, now a healthy ten-month-old baby. When she left, she had no way of knowing that she would never see her son again.

Mary's son, James, as a young child

On their way back to Edinburgh, the royal party was intercepted by Bothwell and his militia. He seized the queen and led her to his castle at Dunbar. If Mary was surprised by the abduction, she did not protest and seemed to go willingly. She remained at Dunbar for two weeks, and during that time she and Bothwell shared the same bed. Mary later described the event by saying that Bothwell's pleadings to marry him were "accompanied none the less by force" until "he has finally driven us to end the work begun at such time and such form as he thought might best serve his turn." In short, when she refused his proposal, he forced himself on her.

When Mary returned to Edinburgh, she had no choice but to marry Bothwell. She had been intimate with him and, according to tradition, must become his wife. Also, Bothwell had convinced her that the lords who had signed the Ainslie Tavern Bond were in support of the marriage.

At the age of twenty-four, Mary, a widow twice over, was married for a third time. The marriage between Mary Queen of Scots and the Earl of Bothwell took place on May 15, 1567, only three months after the murder of Darnley. There were no joyous preparations for the wedding party, and the dispirited queen, once known for her love of clothes, did not even bother to wear a new dress. The wedding was performed according to Protestant rite, proof of how far the queen had fallen under Protestant Bothwell's control. No wedding masques or dancing followed the ceremony, only a dinner in which Mary sat at the head of a long table and Bothwell at the foot.

Mary soon realized the marriage was a mistake. Bothwell began to reveal traits she had not seen before. He was insanely jealous and berated her when she had conversations

Declaration by Lords indicating the Earl of Bothwell as the murderer of Lord Darnley, 1567. *(Courtesy of Bridgeman Art Library)*

with other men. He did not allow her to speak with her lords unless he was present, and he put his men outside her chamber to make sure no one went in without his knowledge. He did not treat her with respect due a wife, let alone a queen, and they argued frequently. Soon her health began to suffer. An observer remarked, "The opinion of many is that the queen is the most changed woman of face that in so little time without extremity of sickness they have seen."

Bothwell was unable to maneuver the shifting loyalties of the Scottish nobles. Not long after the marriage, the same lords who had signed the Ainslie Tavern Bond signed a new bond against Bothwell. Calling themselves the Confederate Lords, they banded together in fear over Bothwell's potential power. In order to justify and obscure their own ambitions, they reopened the case of Darnley's assassination and began to claim that they were morally outraged that the murder, which many of them had been part of, had not been avenged. They charged Bothwell with the crime and called for justice. Furthermore, they insisted that, for the good of Scotland, someone had to rescue the queen from the murderer's evil influence, and they were willing to take on the task if no one else would.

In the early morning hours of June 15, the troops of the Confederate Lords marched from Edinburgh to engage Bothwell in battle. They carried a white banner with an image of Darnley's corpse lying under a green tree. Kneeling beside the body was an infant boy, the young prince, crying out: "Judge and avenge my cause, O Lord."

Bothwell rode with a hastily gathered royal army to meet the Confederate Lords. Mary rode beside him, once again a queen in command, dressed in armor and committed to action. A banner of Scotland's symbol, a red lion, flew overhead. The opposing forces met outside of Edinburgh, with Bothwell's troops camped on Carberry Hill, in what he thought was a strategically advantageous position. Neither side wanted to engage in full-scale battle and attempted to find a way out of the situation. The Lords offered to restore Mary to power if she would turn over Bothwell. She refused, reminding them that they had counseled her to marry Bothwell by signing the Ainslie Tavern Bond.

Bothwell wanted to settle the matter in one-on-one combat, but the nobles could not agree on a challenger. As the day wore on, the sun beat down on the slopes of Carberry Hill and the troops, who had no shelter, began to drift off; soon Mary and Bothwell had no army left.

A sketch of the field at Carberry Hill where Mary and Bothwell surrendered to the Confederate Lords.

Bothwell wanted to stand firm, but there was no course but to surrender. Mary refused to turn over Bothwell, though, and asked the lords to let him ride off safely. They consented, and at sunset Mary and Bothwell said their goodbyes, embracing in front of the troops. It was the last time she ever saw him.

When Mary surrendered, she did not think that she was the focus of the Lords' anger. She assumed that the Lords would escort her back to Holyrood and that in time they would investigate Darnley's murder, exonerate her, and support her as queen. Again, Mary was unable to grasp the treacherous nature of the nobles.

Mary rode toward Edinburgh wearing a scarlet dress, now badly torn, that she had borrowed at Dunbar days earlier. She expected loyalty from her subjects, taking for granted that her people would continue in the support and adoration they had shown her since her early days of rule. But the people had lost trust in her; she had done nothing to show them that she was innocent of the murder of Darnley and the rumors of her adultery with Bothwell had destroyed her reputation. She had behaved in ways that seemed selfish and indulgent. As she was led into Edinburgh, people lined the streets and shouted, "Burn the whore." In her torn red dress, with bedraggled hair and dirty face, Mary did not look like a queen.

Instead of back to Holyrood Palace, the Confederate Lords took Mary to the Lord Provost's home, where she was kept under guard and constantly watched. (The Lord Provost was the head of the civic government, a role similar to mayor.) The next day she was taken to Douglas castle

What remains of Douglas Castle on Lochleven Lake, where Mary Queen of Scots was held captive following the battle at Carberry Hill.

on one of the islands of Lochleven Lake. Confined to this bleak place, Mary had little hope for escape.

Mary did have an unlikely supporter. Queen Elizabeth, concerned at how roughly the nobles were treating a queen, wrote that: "We assure you that whatsoever we can imagine meet for your honour and safety that shall lie in our power, we shall perform the same that it shall well appear you have a good neighbor, a dear sister, and a faithful friend." Elizabeth saw the treatment of Mary by her nobles as a threat to all monarchs. She also felt the vulnerability of a female ruler in a world essentially dominated by men. Mary read into Elizabeth's words sympathy and compassion of one woman for another, and of one cousin for the other.

At Lochleven, the Confederate Lords urged Mary to agree to a divorce from Bothwell, but she refused. She held out hope that he would return and save her. But Bothwell had failed to raise enough troops and was later imprisoned. The Lords then put pressure on Mary to abdicate in favor of her son James. They feared that if Mary were restored to power, she would take action against them. Furthermore, unless Mary abdicated, their actions against her would be seen as a rebellion rather than as pursuit of justice.

Mary was again without someone to trust. She was also ill—it is possible she was pregnant and miscarried, or suffered from the same recurring illness that had caused her to collapse previously during times of stress. Mary's weakened physical condition led her to a fateful action. Under increased pressure, she finally agreed to sign documents issued by the Privy Council stating she was unable to carry out her duties as queen. Mary relinquished the crown to her year old son. She also signed a document designating her half-brother James,

James Stewart, the Earl of Moray, and Mary's half brother

the Earl of Moray, as regent during James's minority. Five days later Mary's son became James VI of Scotland.

James, Earl of Moray, returned to Scotland from England. At last he was to have the power he had so long coveted. As regent, he would rule Scotland for years before James VI came of age. When Moray arrived at Lochleven to assume his duties, he angrily denounced Mary to her face for her behavior with Bothwell and taunted her saying that her reputation was ruined. He insisted on taking her jewelry, and made her wear clothes unfit for a queen.

Mary did not give up though. She was convinced that she could rely on the help of many loyal supporters on the mainland and thus began to plan her escape and the recovery of her power. Once freed, she could claim that the abdication had been forced upon her by threat of death.

Mary had help close by. Two young men from the Douglas family had become infatuated with her. During her imprisonment, one of them, George Douglas, began corresponding with Mary's friends and making arrangements for her escape. Ten and a half months after her capture, she was ready to escape with George's help.

Disguised in the red cloak of one of her attendants, Mary walked through the castle gate, unlocked earlier by young Willie Douglas with a stolen key. Willie had also tied together all the boats in the harbor to slow down pursuit. Under darkness, Mary was smuggled into a boat and rowed to shore, where friends and supporters, led by Lord Seton, met her with horses. She began rallying support and troops.

Meanwhile, the Confederate Lords, headed by Moray, were in pursuit. Mary decided to attack their army before they could get reinforcements. However, despite the surprise attack and her superior number of men, Moray's troops were more experienced and better disciplined. Defeated, Mary fled the battlefield.

Then, she made a crucial mistake. Her advisors urged her to seek help from France, Scotland's traditional ally and the home of her mother's powerful family. But Mary ignored their counsel and, clinging to the empathy she had sensed in Elizabeth's letter, decided to seek refuge in England. She hoped Elizabeth would supply her with troops, even though her advisors pointed out that Elizabeth had sheltered Moray and continued to correspond with him. Most importantly, they pointed out, Mary posed a threat to Elizabeth's hold on the English throne. She could hardly be expected to welcome her rival with open arms.

But Mary was determined. She wrote to Elizabeth, asking for safe passage to England, but did not wait for an answer. On May 16, disguised as a commoner, and with a small band of supporters, including George and Willie Douglas, Mary boarded a fishing boat and crossed the Solway River into England.

8

No More Ado About Her

Mary hoped to have an audience with Queen Elizabeth; she hoped to persuade her cousin to renounce the rebellious Scottish lords and help her to reclaim her throne.

In London, however, Elizabeth was dismayed when she learned of Mary's arrival in England. She believed the Scottish nobles were guilty of treason, but little was to be gained if she sent Mary back to Scotland, even with an armed force, when it was clear the nobles did not want her returned. However, Elizabeth could not let Mary remain free in England, where the Catholic religion was still strong, especially in the north, and there was the ever-present danger that the Catholic English nobles would rally around Mary. Bringing Mary to London

Mary fled to Elizabeth in England in hopes of gaining her cousin's help to reclaim the Scottish throne. *(National Portrait Gallery, London)*

was also out of the question; Elizabeth was not prepared to meet her cousin and rival face-to-face.

Mary failed to understand the position she had placed Elizabeth in by coming to England. While Mary had become increasingly impulsive, Elizabeth, who had been impetuous as a young woman, had matured. Her head usually ruled her heart, and she was capable of ruthlessness if she thought it necessary—and in this instance, she did. Elizabeth had Mary imprisoned, on the grounds of being an accomplice in the murder of her husband. This was possible because the governing lords in Scotland had publicly accused Mary of complicity in the crime.

Mary was confined to Carlisle Castle two days after arriving in northern England. Outraged at her treatment, she wrote letters to Elizabeth begging for help. She railed against the men who had conspired to kill Darnley and were now accusing her of their crime. In letters to the Cardinal of Lorraine and her other Guise relatives, Mary complained of her treatment, saying the food was meager and luxuries nonexistent. Her castle was dark and dank and instead of forty ladies-in-waiting she now had only two or three women of low rank to attend her. There were grates on the windows, and soldiers swarmed outside her rooms. When she walked on the grounds, a guard of one hundred men escorted her. She was treated like a caged animal, and bristled with a desire for revenge.

Despite her anger, Mary still had the power to charm. Sir Francis Knollys, Elizabeth's trusted counselor, acted as keeper and soon was infatuated with Mary, calling her a "notable woman" and extolling her intelligence, wit, and tolerance. Mary had arrived in England with only the clothes on her back, and Knollys implored Elizabeth to send her a wardrobe.

Elizabeth ordered Mary to be imprisoned at Carlisle Castle shortly after she reached the English shores.

He sympathized with Mary's indignant reaction to the inferior quality of the dresses Elizabeth sent.

Both Elizabeth and Moray realized they could not keep Mary imprisoned indefinitely without trial. There had to be a resolution of the charges against her. Moray and the King's Men, as the supporters of James VI were called, accused Mary of adultery with Bothwell, of collusion in her abduction by him, and of complicity in the murder of Darnley. Mary insisted she was innocent of these charges and that there was no evidence against her. She claimed the lords had acted in their own self-interest and unlawfully forced her to give up the throne.

In June, a month after Mary's arrival in northern England, Moray announced to Elizabeth that he had irrefutable proof of Mary's guilt. He told Elizabeth that he would procure copies of letters translated from French into Scottish that had been written by Mary to Bothwell, and that the letters would prove her guilt on all the charges.

Before Moray produced the letters, he insisted that Elizabeth agree if Mary were found guilty, she would not be allowed to return to Scotland. The only way he could maintain his power was to keep his half-sister out of the country. Elizabeth was reluctant, but agreed. Meanwhile, Elizabeth continued to assure Mary that if she would consent to a judgment, she personally would guarantee that Mary was restored to the Scottish throne no matter what the outcome of the hearing. Encouraged, Mary agreed to the trial, convinced that her restoration as queen of Scots was imminent.

Elizabeth convened a conference at York in October, 1568, to examine the evidence. Three English judges, headed by the Duke of Norfolk, Elizabeth's most powerful nobleman, presided over the trial. Moray and Mary each had commissioners to defend their claims. When Moray presented the letters from Mary to Bothwell, two of the judges appeared indifferent to their contents, but Norfolk wanted to show the letters to Elizabeth to ask her advice. This request, thought inappropriate by many because Norfolk clearly wanted to get instruction on what to do from Elizabeth, caused a great deal of controversy, and the conference ended inconclusively.

One month later, Elizabeth called a new conference at Westminster. Mary requested to attend to answer her half-brother's accusations, but Elizabeth refused. The tribunal was expanded to include several English judges as well as the commissioners who represented Mary. Moray again presented his evidence. This time he produced a small, silver casket and said it had been found among Bothwell's belongings at

The Duke of Norfolk, Elizabeth's most powerful nobleman, presided over the trial of Mary Queen of Scots for conspiracy in the murder of her husband, Lord Darnley.

Holyrood. Of chief importance were eight letters he said it had contained, known as the Casket Letters, which Moray claimed Mary had written to Bothwell. The letters proclaimed her passionate love for him and her desire to be free of a miserable marriage. The letters were offered as conclusive proof that Mary was not only carrying on an adulterous love affair with

Bothwell, but also that she had conspired with him to kill Darnley and later colluded in her own abduction.

One letter mentioned that the writer would "bring the man" to Craigmillar, a reference that Moray claimed revealed that Mary had lured Darnley to his death. One request for "some invention more secret by physick" suggested that the murder plot included poison. The letter was sent "from Glasgow this Saturday" where Mary was visiting Darnley's sick bed. The second letter spoke of a sick man whose breath was "worse than your uncle's," a possible description of Darnley's bout with syphilis, and complained of not hearing from the loved one and made declarations of passion. In the third letter a reference to a secret "marriage" of bodies was presented as proof of an adulterous relationship.

With notations at the top of each letter stating the incriminating evidence drawn from the contents, the letters built the picture of a woman passionately in love and desperate to be rid of an unwanted husband.

Mary was not permitted to see the letters, but she vehemently denied their authenticity and insisted that had she seen the letters the result would have been "to the declaration of my innocence and confusion of their falsity." Her supporters presented several objections to the letters. First, not one was an original, so it was impossible to prove that Mary was the author. Secondly, none of the letters were dated or contained either an addressee or closing signature. Furthermore, each of the letters had phrases written in different hands and unexplainable blank spaces between lines. Upon close examination, it could be seen that, while parts of the letter may have been written by Mary, the time, recipient, and circumstances were not as Moray claimed.

For instance, in the first letter, the only thing suggesting that it had been written while Mary was visiting Darnley before the murder, as Moray claimed, was the phrase, "This Saturday from Glascow." That phrase, however, was written in a distinctly different hand from the rest of the letter—possibly it had been added later. The reference to poison failed to be incriminating, because poison was never part of the Darnley murder plot.

The conference ended on January 11, 1569, without a conclusive result. Mary had not been found guilty of the crimes charged against her, but neither had she been found innocent.

During the proceedings, Mary again found a man to help her. The widowed Duke of Norfolk, the chief judge at the Conference at York, had decided Mary would make a suitable wife, and he had begun secret negotiations to arrange the marriage. Norfolk was one of Elizabeth's most influential dukes, but his family was at the center of the Catholic party in England. He saw marriage to Mary as a way to put himself and Mary on the English throne, with the help of the Catholics.

Mary began to pin her hopes on Norfolk. She wrote to the pope, asking him to annul her marriage to Bothwell on the grounds that since the wedding was performed by Protestant rites it was not valid in the eyes of the Catholic Church. She wrote love letters to Norfolk, even though she had never met him. She declared, "I will live and die with you." When Norfolk sent Mary a diamond, she replied, "As you please command me; for I will for all the world follow your commandment." Mary, eager to be set free, was willing to enter into marriage with Norfolk without any reservations.

As had been true so often in the past, Mary's behavior was naive and impulsive. No one had told Elizabeth of the proposed marriage between Mary and Norfolk, and without her consent, the union could not occur. It was Moray who shrewdly revealed Norfolk's marriage plan to Elizabeth—he sent her a copy of the certified letter Norfolk had written to him declaring his intention of wedding Mary.

Elizabeth knew that after marrying the influential Norfolk, Mary would seek to regain her position as queen of Scotland, and Norfolk would pursue his wife's claim to the throne of England. She was furious, and she had the duke thrown into the Tower of London.

Even as Mary hoped for a marriage to Norfolk, she began investigating other plots that might aid in her return to Scotland. She gave up hope, too late, that Elizabeth would help her, and believed her only chance for freedom would come from the restoration of Catholicism in England. She wrote to King Philip of Spain and declared herself a devoted daughter of the Catholic Church. Through Norfolk's connections, Mary arranged to transfer money to a Florentine banker named Roberto di Ridolfi who was heading a movement to force Elizabeth to return England to Catholicism.

Ridolfi proceeded to draw up a plan to depose Elizabeth, a plot called the Enterprise Against England, and to present it to King Philip in hopes of getting his support. The plan was to capture Elizabeth as she traveled to a new summer residence; hopefully, this would then incite an uprising of English Catholics, who would free Mary and hasten her marriage to Norfolk. A Spanish fleet would then land and secure the country, and Mary and Norfolk would ascend to the throne.

William Cecil, Elizabeth's trusted secretary, foiled Mary's plans to capture her cousin.

Unfortunately, details of this bold and idealistic plot were intercepted by an English spy and sent directly to Elizabeth's Secretary, and Mary's old nemesis, William Cecil, who had been wary of Mary and her claim to the throne for years. Meanwhile, another of Mary's old enemies, John Knox, wrote to Cecil, a fellow Protestant, advising him to order Mary's death at once, for "if ye strike not at the root, the branches that appear to be broken will bud again."

Cecil wanted to take Knox's advice but, to his great frustration, he had no real evidence of Mary's involvement in the plan to depose Elizabeth. The most incriminating letter he had from her urged deliverance of afflicted Catholics from bondage and the defense of the rightful prince by "cutting of the most faithless antichrist and usurper of titles, the destroyer of justice, the persecutor of God and his church." But Mary never specifically mentioned Elizabeth or Philip or the plot, and Cecil had no grounds to bring her to trial for treason.

Still, Cecil desperately wanted to have Mary executed. Ever since Mary's return to Scotland from France, Cecil had seen the Scottish queen as a threat to Elizabeth. He agreed with John Knox that Mary deserved to die and that the Catholics were spinning plots. In Rome, Pope Pius V, who hoped to reverse the English Reformation and had declared Queen Elizabeth only a "pretender" to the throne, released her subjects from allegiance to her. Cecil countered by declaring that Catholics were traitors. He drafted bills excluding Catholics from Parliament and drafted another bill disqualifying any candidate for succession who at any time for the remainder of Elizabeth's life tried to claim the throne.

Popular opinion in England was also against Mary, where she was viewed as a foreign-born Catholic who had plotted against the English Protestant queen. The involvement of the Catholic Guises in the St. Bartholomew's Day Massacre on August 24, 1572, in which some three thousand French Protestants were slaughtered in Paris, added to Mary's unpopularity.

Cecil decided the time was right to make public the case that had been presented against Mary, despite the fact that Elizabeth herself wanted the information kept private. He arranged for the publication of translations of the letters. He then used the unproven accusations against Mary to suggest she was a murderess and adulteress, and probably involved

The deaths of some 3,000 French protestants in the St. Bartholomew's Day Massacre only made matters worse for Mary.

as a co-conspirator in the Enterprise Against England plot.

The translated letters were circulated widely. When Parliament assembled in 1572 to discuss Elizabeth's safety, speaker after speaker called for Mary's execution. "Cut off her head and make no more ado about her," was the general feeling.

Elizabeth refused to order the execution. It was not legally possible to convict the anointed Queen of Scots of treason in England. Furthermore, she refused to sign a bill barring Mary from the English succession. The only thing she agreed to do was have Norfolk executed. Cecil, angry and frustrated, vowed to have Mary excluded from succession in any way he could. Over the next decade, Cecil worked to piece together a trap for Mary to fall into.

9

Captivity

Mary remained a prisoner of Queen Elizabeth for the next fifteen and a half years. She was moved periodically from one castle to another, but always under guard, and she was pulled between hope of freedom and despair that she'd spend the rest of her life imprisoned by her cousin, Queen Elizabeth.

In 1569, Cecil ordered her to be taken to Tutbury Castle in the Midlands of England, where she was cut off from rescue by sea and isolated from her sympathizers in the north. The castle was dreary and dilapidated, and poor drainage made the interior damp and filled it with constant, noxious odors. Mary soon fell ill. She later wrote about how the winter winds blew into every corner of her wood and plaster chamber. Her warden, the Earl of Shrewsbury, negotiated with Elizabeth to

Mary spent part of her captivity at Tutbury Castle.

move Mary to a more comfortable residence in the center of England. Over the next eleven years Mary moved back and forth between Sheffield Castle and Sheffield Manor, with summer visits to a lodge Shrewsbury built for her near the spa at Buxton.

The Earl of Shrewsbury had been chosen to be her warden because of his unquestioned loyalty to Elizabeth. As Mary's jailer, he was always concerned with Elizabeth's reactions to his decisions, but still worked to make sure that even if Mary was not free, she was comfortable. A wealthy man, he paid for much of Mary's household expenses out of his own pocket, though not without complaint. Throughout her years with Shrewsbury, Mary was treated honorably, and had her own staff of cooks, laundresses, and attendants. She even kept her own horses, though she was not allowed to ride often or far. When reductions in her household were ordered, Mary made sure that pensions were arranged from her French income for the laid-off servants.

Mary's chamber and antechamber were made comfortable: tapestries hung on the walls, Turkish carpets lined the floors, and she was allowed some visitors. During these years she adopted her mother's motto: "In my end is my beginning." The motto proclaimed her conviction that, even if she were killed, her dynastic claim to the throne of England would live on through her son James.

Mary's canopied bed was made with fresh linen sheets each day, and she continued to dress like a reigning queen. She asked her agent in Paris to send her "pattern of dresses, and of cloth of gold and silver, and of silks the handsomest and the rarest that are worn at court." When she switched castles, it took thirty carts to carry all her possessions. Mary Seton, the only one of the Four Marys to be with her in England, dressed Mary's hair. During her escape from the Scottish rebels, Mary had cut off almost all of her hair and it never grew back in abundance. Mary Seton incorporated false hairpieces into elaborate hairstyles: "She did set such a curled hair upon the queen that was said to be a periwig that showed very delicately."

Mary followed the rituals of royal eating, consisting of two courses for both dinner and supper. She chose from nearly thirty-two dishes daily, mostly meat except for fish on Fridays and during Lent. Dinner, served between eleven in the morning and noon, would consist of a first course of soup, veal, beef, mutton, pork, capon, goose, duck, and rabbit, followed by a

During the first part of her captivity, Mary spent time with the Earl of Shrewsbury's wife, Bess of Hardwick.

second course of pheasant, partridge, kid lamb, quail, pigeon, tart and frittered apples or pears. Supper, served between five and six during the winter and seven to eight during the summer, consisted of similar meat and fowl dishes. The food was served on silver dishes and wine was poured into crystal goblets. Not allowed to exercise as she had in Scotland, Mary began to put on weight. Her chin softened into fullness, her shoulders rounded, and she developed a slight stoop.

In the early years of her captivity Mary spent many hours in the company of Shrewsbury's wife. Bess of Hardwick, more than twenty years Mary's senior, was a selfish, ambitious, jealous woman and incurable gossip. Bess and Mary embroidered together, a pastime Mary grew to enjoy. Embroidering became

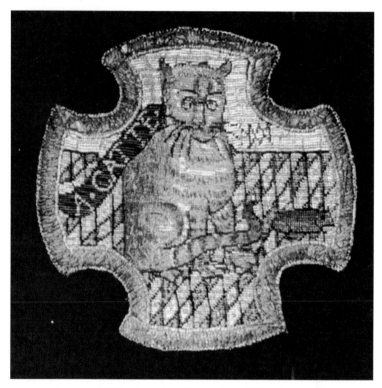

In this picture of Mary's embroidery, she stitched an orange cat to represent Queen Elizabeth, and a mouse to represent herself.

a way for Mary to express her feelings, specifically the anger she felt toward Elizabeth. One of her works shows an orange cat looming over a cornered mouse. Elizabeth, with her red hair, was the cat, Mary the captured mouse.

Mary continued to suffer episodes of intense illness. Shortly after being moved to Tutbury, she suffered another attack of vomiting and nausea. Again, the doctor resorted to purging—that seemed to give some relief. Alarmed, Shrewsbury negotiated with Elizabeth to have two physicians on standby. Mary also suffered from a chronic pain in her left side and her legs became swollen, making it difficult to walk.

She also suffered from periods of depression, worsening her physical problems. She proclaimed, "No one can cure this malady as well as the queen of England." Some relief came when she was allowed to visit the baths at Buxton, where the mineral waters soothed her discomfort. Shrewsbury built a lodge at Buxton and Mary spent summers there for several years. The baths also gave Mary an opportunity to see people, although her communication with them was curtailed. Mary held out hope that Elizabeth herself would come to the baths, but it never happened.

During Mary's imprisonment, Scotland was consumed by warring factions, all vying for regency and control of the Scottish dynasty while her son King James VI was too young to rule. In 1570, Mary's treacherous half-brother, James Stewart, Lord Moray, was assassinated by a member

The Earl of Morton

of the rival Hamilton clan. King James VI's grandfather Lennox became the new regent, but his rule was cut short by his death a year later. Then the Earl of Morton, who had never been a friend to Mary, was named regent. Sanctioned by Elizabeth, he attacked the castle of Edinburgh, long held by Mary's supporters in the hope that she would escape and reclaim her throne. Mary's hopes of restoration with Elizabeth's help ended.

Mary continued to correspond with her Guise relatives, her former brother-in-law, Charles IX, and the officials of the French embassy in London. But to Mary's dismay, her grandmother, the same woman who had exerted such an influence over her as a child, refused to communicate with her. Antoinette could not forgive Mary for entering into two unwise marriages. For some time Mary held out hope that her former mother-in-law Catherine de' Medici and her son Charles IX would come to her aid, and she devised a secret code to communicate with Charles.

But Mary did not know that all her letters were being intercepted and sent on to agents of Elizabeth's new principal secretary, Sir Francis Walsingham, who was Cecil's protégé, as well as a spy. After the letters were copied for Walsingham and Cecil, they were sent on to their recipients.

When her uncle, the Cardinal of Lorraine, died in 1574, Mary discovered that her younger generation of cousins did not sympathize with her cause. Growing desperate, Mary looked more and more to Spain, a long-time enemy of England, and Philip's plan for making Europe Catholic again.

The best hope for Mary's release lay in her son James, who was little more than a year old when Mary fled to England. She wrote to him expressing her love, but Elizabeth would

Sir Francis Walsingham, a protégé of Cecil, spied on Mary.

not allow the letters to be sent. In her mind Mary believed that James must long for her as much as she longed for him, and sympathetic visitors assured her of her son's belief in her innocence. But the truth was that James Stewart, the Earl of Moray, before his assassination, had thoroughly turned the young king against his mother. James had been taught that his mother was both an adulterer and a murderer.

James had been brought up as a ruling monarch. However, in her brief freedom before she fled Scotland, Mary had revoked the abdication she had made under pressure from the nobles. In her mind, and in the minds of her supporters, she was still the true queen of Scotland. In 1581, Mary proposed a plan for her and James to rule jointly. Naturally, this involved her return to Scotland. James pretended to be interested in the plan, while at the same time trying to negotiate his succession to the English crown in a scheme that did not include the release of Mary. When James finally rejected his mother's plan, Mary was devastated at this ultimate betrayal.

Mary's son, James, who did not come to his mother's aid

By the 1580s, the polarization of the Catholics and the Protestants in Europe was approaching a climax. War between England and Spain seemed inevitable, putting pressure on Elizabeth to prevent Mary from aligning with Spanish King Philip. At Cecil's instigation, Parliament enacted the Act for the Queen's Safety, which promised execution for anyone who plotted against Elizabeth. A far more dangerous clause ordered the execution of anyone in whose favor plots might be instigated, whether or not they were involved. In other words, if a Catholic conspiracy to kill Elizabeth and put Mary on the English throne were discovered, Mary could be tried and executed even if she was ignorant of the plot. One of the obvious intents of the law was to make it easier to find a way to execute Mary. Ominously, Elizabeth did not try to block the act from passing in Parliament.

In 1584, in order to isolate her further, Mary was returned to Tutbury, this time into the custody of a man named Paulet, who was her sole keeper for the next two years. Bess had accused her husband, Shrewsbury, of having an affair with Mary. Mary defended herself by recounting to Elizabeth the gossip Bess had spread about her. The outcome of all this was a divorce between Shrewsbury and his wife, and the end of Shrewsbury's custody of Mary.

Paulet was a pitiless man, completely unmoved by Mary's charm and her plight. Whenever he entered her antechamber, he tore down the cloth of state from over her chair. He opened her letters, always on the look out for her involvement in a conspiracy. Mary was more isolated than ever before. Her secret pipeline, through which she corresponded with her foreign agents, was shut off and she was deprived of any news of the outside world.

In the winter of 1585, Mary was moved to Chartley Hall, an Elizabethan manor house surrounded by a large moat. She became so ill that for nearly three months she was confined to her bed and her servants feared for her life.

Mary was desperate. Her temperament was such that she could not refrain from actively seeking escape. Action had always been preferable to inaction, and she began to recklessly pursue escape plots, regardless of how rash they were. Her unrelenting illness and pain further clouded her judgment. Cecil, sensing that Mary was finally about to incriminate herself, had the spy Walsingham begin to set a trap.

Early in 1586, a young Catholic named Gilbert Gifford came to Chartley Hall. Mary was delighted to have a Catholic in her household and allowed herself to be swayed by his support for her cause. The truth, though, was that the formerly Catholic Gifford had secretly converted to Protestantism, and been sent by Walsingham to spy on Mary, and if possible, lead her into a plot against Elizabeth.

Gifford suggested a scheme to sneak letters in and out of Chartley. Mary dictated letters to her secretary, who put them into a code that was set up between Mary and her correspondents in the first letters she wrote. Her secretary wrapped the letters in a leather packet and gave them to the Chartley brewer, who had moved with his family to the town next to Chartley Hall. The brewer slipped the packet through a corked tube in the opening of the beer cask. The process was reversed for Mary to receive her secret mail. Through this mail system, Mary renewed her schemes for rescue through the aid of France or Spain.

Mary was told the letters were being sent to the French embassy in London, and from there on to Paris. But, in actuality, the brewer delivered the letters to Gifford, who took them to Walsingham to be decoded and copied before sending them on to the French embassy.

Then another important development took place. Sir Anthony Babington was a member of a new generation of Catholics who had grown up in England to believe that Mary embodied the goodness of Catholicism and was being held hostage by Protestantism. Babington had been a page to Shrewsbury, and during his years of service had become entranced with the captive queen. Rich and charismatic, he decided in 1586 that he and his companions would rescue

Mary, remove Elizabeth from her throne, and make Mary Queen of England.

It was no coincidence that Gifford, who was also in touch with Babington, recommended the young man to Mary as a trustworthy contact. Babington's plot was now connected to Mary's desperation for an escape, and the trap was set. Mary wrote to Babington, and in his reply he disclosed the particulars of his plan: an invasion from abroad would be joined by English Catholic sympathizers. Mary would be freed and there would be a "despatch of the usurping Competitor," meaning Elizabeth would be killed. Babington promised that he and ten of his friends would rescue Mary, while six noble gentlemen from among his friends would attend to the "Competitor."

Mary's secretary, sensing at worst a trap but at best another disastrous scheme, advised her against writing back to Babington. But Mary was desperate and had grown increasingly despondent. Devastated by her son's betrayal and her own isolation, she wanted only to "retire out of this island in some solitary and reposeful place, as much for her soul as for her body."

In July 1586, Mary had learned of a treaty of alliance between her son James and Queen Elizabeth that totally excluded her interests. Her only solace would be to escape. The prospect of freedom overcame any caution. She wrote a long letter to Babington approving the details of his plan. She made no protest against the assassination of Elizabeth, and only concentrated on the details of her own rescue. She conveyed to Babington the necessity for secrecy and the terrible consequences that would befall her should the plot be discovered. Finally, she reminded him of the need for "a good army" to rescue her. When Walsingham's agent received

Mary's letter to Babington, he drew a gallows on the envelope of the copy he sent on to Cecil.

Mary's hopes were high in the late summer of 1586. August 11 was a beautiful day, and Paulet surprised her by asking her if she would like to ride out with him to a buck hunt. Mary was thrilled and took great care in dressing, thinking that she would be meeting some of the local gentry. Her secretaries and personal physician joined the small party.

As they made their way across the moors, Paulet lagged behind. Suddenly, in the distance, Mary saw a band of horsemen riding fast toward them. She hoped it was the foreign army promised by Babington, but the first words from the leader of the group dashed those hopes: "Madame, the Queen my mistress finds it very strange that you, contrary to the pact and engagement made between you, should have conspired against her and her state."

Mary's protests were futile. Her secretaries were taken away; she would never see them again. She sat on the ground and refused to move until Paulet threatened to use force. Before proceeding, she knelt under a tree to pray.

For the next two weeks Mary was kept at a manor house in Taixell. At Chartley, her belongings were searched and all her correspondence and belongings seized. She begged Paulet to let her use her money to send her servants back to France. But Paulet refused and the money was seized.

Babington and his fellow conspirators were executed. Mary's secretaries had been shown a facsimile of her original letter and had testified that it was in her hand. On September 21, she was taken out of Chartley and began a four day journey to Fotheringhay Castle to stand trial for treason against the Queen of England.

10

A Queen Condemned

O ver the two weeks between her arrest and her removal from Chartley, Mary changed. Those who saw her noticed a new serenity. She seemed to have accepted her fate and was determined to die a public martyr to the Catholic faith. She wanted to give testimony to her religious beliefs and proclaimed, "For myself, I am resolute to die for my religion."

Fotheringhay was a huge castle with grim towers that rose over the surrounding countryside. Commissioners and peers came from London to participate in Mary's trial. She expressed relief that she would not be killed secretly, which would have robbed her of an audience for her martyrdom.

The provisions of the Act for the Queen's Safety left no chance of acquittal. At the trial Mary was to have neither counsel nor witnesses to appear in her defense. When Cecil came to her chamber to inform her of the trial, she proclaimed that she would not appear. "I am a queen and not a subject. If I appeared, I should betray the dignity and majesty of kings and it would be tantamount to a confession that I am bound to submit to the laws of England, even in matters of religion." She was willing to be interrogated by Parliament but not before commissioners whose minds were already set against her. She continued to reiterate her objections to the illegality of the trial and warned Cecil, "Look to your consciences and remember that the theater of the world is wider than the realm of England."

Cecil declared that the trial would proceed and if Mary did not appear she would be condemned in absentia. She finally agreed to appear in order to answer the charge that she had plotted the assassination of Elizabeth. In agreeing to stand trial, Mary gave up her royal position, but what she gained was time in the "theatre of the world."

The trial of Mary Queen of Scots began in October 1586. She was brought into the great hall under an escort of soldiers. She wore a black dress and mantle, a white headdress, and a long, white veil, but was so lame with rheumatism that she had to be assisted on both arms.

Although demeaned from the beginning, Mary maintained her composure. The court was set up with a throne on a dais, but she was led to a red velvet chair at the side. The empty throne was a symbol of the authority of Elizabeth, who was not present. During the trial, all speeches were addressed to the lords, so Mary had to interrupt them if she wanted to make a point. Evidence was presented in no particular order, confusing Mary, who had not been given a chance to review it ahead of time. Nevertheless, she remained calm. The woman who had so often been incapable of acting without the advice of others now relied completely upon herself.

The key evidence presented was the copies of the correspondence between Mary and Babington. Mary argued that this secondhand evidence could easily have been tampered with and demanded to see the originals, but they were not produced. The evidence of Mary's secretaries was also examined. She questioned why they were not present as witnesses and insinuated their absence cast doubt on their depositions. Her secretary could have added to her letter as he translated it into code. However, she said, "For my part, I do not wish to accuse."

Mary argued that she never met Babington and that her connection to him was based on her own desire for freedom, not on any plan to overthrow Elizabeth. She made clear her lack of political ambition: "My advancing age and bodily weakness both prevent me from wishing to resume the reins of government."

In reality though, Mary was on trial for much more than her involvement in the Babington plot. Cecil finally had her cornered and wanted to try Mary for all the crimes he thought she had committed. He condemned her for having taken up against English arms at the time of her French marriage, when France and England had been at war, presenting it as her intention to usurp Elizabeth's throne. Mary replied that she had been very young and had acted in obedience to her father-in-law, Henry II of France. Cecil then went on to criticize Mary's refusal to ratify the Treaty of Edinburgh. Mary replied that a queen should never be expected to cede her rights without concessions. She had never wished to usurp the throne while Elizabeth lived, but would not relinquish her right to the succession. Later in the trial, when Cecil accused Mary of planning to kill Elizabeth, Mary exclaimed, "Ah, you are indeed my adversary."

Throughout the trial Mary maintained repeatedly, "I desired nothing but my own deliverance." She also acknowledged her support of the Catholic cause in England. She had not sought the Pope's proclamation of Elizabeth as a Pretender, but she would not contradict it.

Rising from her chair at the conclusion of the trial, Mary faced the assembly. With all of her regal presence she pardoned them and added, "My lords and gentlemen, I place my cause in the hands of God." She had conducted herself with poise and shown cleverness and intelligence in conducting her defense. But the outcome was forgone before the trial began: Mary's death sentence was handed down at the end of October. After nineteen years of captivity, her escape would be brought on by an untimely death.

It was four months before the execution was carried out. Elizabeth first had to confirm Mary's sentence, but she had difficulty bringing herself to do so. She feared the repercussions of executing a queen and wanted either a confession from Mary or for Parliament to find some way to spare her life. She even went so far as to suggest that if Mary were killed by a private citizen, there would be no reprisals.

As Mary awaited her death, she took comfort in her new role as Catholic martyr. Her religion had new meaning for her and she professed to having found a new inner peace.

On the evening of February 7, 1587, three earls, Shrewsbury among them, approached Mary's private chamber and informed her that she was to be executed at eight o'clock the next morning. Mary received the news calmly, and when the warrant had been read, she said, "I thank you for such welcome news. You will do me great good in withdrawing me from this world out of which I am very glad to go."

She was not allowed to see her own chaplain, but during the night wrote him a letter containing her confession. She spent her last evening with her servants, the men and women with whom she had bonded over the years of her imprisonment. She stayed up until two in the morning, sorting her belongings and writing letters, distributing packets of money to her servants, and setting aside mementos for relatives abroad. She wrote a will that made provisions for her servants and made charitable bequests for the poor children of Rheims, France, the burial place of her mother.

In a letter to Elizabeth written hours before her death, Mary asked her to "permit my poor desolated servants . . . to carry away my corpse, to bury it in holy ground, with the other queens of France." Her last letter was to her brother-in-law, King Henry III of France. It conveyed her belief that it was her religion and her place in the English succession that were the true causes of her execution.

At six o'clock, after a sleepless night, Mary began to dress. Her outer garments were black, except for the long white veil edged in lace, and the white peaked headdress partially covering her auburn hair. Sometime after eight, a messenger shouted through the door that the lords were waiting. Mary was escorted to the great hall in Fotheringhay, where a scaffold had been erected and hung with black. A stage had also been placed, about twelve feet square, also hung with black. Mary turned her face away when the Protestant dean began to pray. When he was finished she prayed out loud for the

The last letter that Mary wrote before her execution was to her brother-in-law, King Henry III of France.

proteste de la recepuoir innocente et ... taxé et .....
quant ie seroie leur jubiecte la religion chatolique
et le maynetieu du droit que dieu ma donne a
ceste couronne sont les deulx poincts de ma
condampnation et toutesfoys ilz ne me veullent
permettre de dire que cest pour la religion catholique
que ie meurs mays pour la crainte du champffe
de la feur et pour preuue ilz mont oste mon
aulmonier lequel bien quil soit en la mayson ie
nay peu obtenir quil me viost confesser ny
communier a ma mort mays mont faict grande
instance de recepuoir la consolation et doctrine
de leur ministre ammene pour ce faict ce porteur
et sa compaignie la pluspart de vos subiectz
vous termoigneront mes desportemantz en ce
dineu acte dernier il reste que ie vous suphie
comme roy tres chrestien mon beau frere et ansien
allyé et qui mauuez tousiours proteste de
maymer qua ce coup vous fussiez preuue en
toutz ces poincts de vostre vertu tant par
charité me soulageant de ce que pour deschar
ger ma consceance ie ne puis sans vous qui
est de recompenser mes seruiteurs desoléz leur

Mary Queen of Scots being led to her execution.

afflicted Catholic Church, for her son, and for Elizabeth. When the executioners tried to dismiss her servants, Mary persuaded them to let six of them attend her death. Not only did she not want to be alone in her final minutes, but she also wanted witnesses to her death to tell her story.

Her women helped her to remove her outer clothes until she stood in a dark red petticoat and bodice, the color red signifying the blood she would spill for the Catholic cause. One attendant covered her eyes with a white cloth and then wrapped her hair and head, leaving only her neck exposed.

The forty-four-year-old Queen of Scotland was ready. Showing no fear, she knelt by the block and, after feeling for it with her hand, laid her head upon it and uttered the words, "Into your hands O Lord I commend my spirit." The executioner missed his mark on the first blow and hit the back of her head. The next blow severed her head.

When the executioner picked up her head by the hair to display it, the skull fell, leaving the executioner holding a red wig. The head, covered in short gray hair, rolled to a stop on the ground beside the body. A small dog, Mary's favorite, hidden in her skirts, ran out to lie down by the head, whimpering.

At one o'clock, Shrewsbury's oldest son galloped forth from Fotheringhay to inform Elizabeth that her orders had

The execution of Mary Queen of Scots

been carried out and Mary was dead. When she heard the news, Elizabeth expressed distress until Cecil reminded her that she should be calm. Mary's supporters might seize on her reaction as evidence that Elizabeth was guilty because Mary had been executed unlawfully.

In the streets of London most people rejoiced at news of the death of the Queen of Scots, whom they had been led to believe was a threat to Elizabeth and to the Protestant religion. In France the news was received with national mourning for the dowager queen. In Scotland, James expressed little emotion over the death of the mother he'd never known. The people, however, expressed the anger that James suppressed.

On July 30, 1587, Queen Mary's body was taken from Fotheringhay and placed in a vault in the cathedral at Peterborough in a Protestant ceremony. In 1612, James was persuaded to honor his mother by having her body removed from its vault and placed in a tomb in Westminster Abbey in London. Mary, who cared so much about the English succession, found her place at last among the kings and queens of England.

In 1603, her son James ascended the throne of England, thus ruling over the two countries as James VI of Scotland and James I of England. Although Mary herself never attained her dream of ruling England, her line of succession survived. The words of her motto proved true: "In my end is my beginning."

Timeline

1542 Mary Stuart (originally Stewart) is born at Linlithgow Palace on December 8; father, King James V of Scotland, dies at Falkland Palace on December 14; six-day-old Mary becomes Queen of Scotland.

1543 Crowned Queen of Scots at Stirling Castle.

1544 Francis, son of future King Henry II of France born.

1548 Sails for France to live with Henry II and his family.

1558 Marries Francis at Notre Dame Cathedral in Paris on April 24.

1559 King Henry II of France dies; Francis becomes king and Mary queen.

1560 Mother, Marie de Guise, dies in Scotland; husband dies on December 5.

1561 Arrives back in Scotland.

1565 Marries Lord Darnley; leads troops in The Chaseabout Raid against Scottish rebels; becomes pregnant.

1566 Secretary David Riccio murdered; Mary gives birth to son, James.

1567 Travels to Glasgow and convinces Darnley to return to Edinburgh; on February 10, Lord Darnley is assassinated at Kirk o' Field; Lord Bothwell is tried and acquitted of murder of Darnley; Bothwell convinces several nobles to sign Ainslie Tavern Bond, a document that supports Bothwell's plan to marry Mary; Bothwell abducts Mary, takes her to Dunbar Castle; Mary marries Bothwell at Carberry Hill; Bothwell and Mary engage in a confrontation with troops of the Confederate Lords, are defeated, and Bothwell flees; Mary returns to Edinburgh, is placed under house arrest, abdicates the throne; son is crowned James VI, King of Scotland, at Stirling Castle.

1568 Escapes to England, confined to Carlisle Castle; requests aid from Queen Elizabeth; conference to determine guilt in conspiracy to kill Darnley begins.

1569 Conference concludes without a resolution.

1586 Moved from castle to castle, living under house arrest as prisoner of Elizabeth.

1586 Babington Plot is uncovered and conspirators executed; Mary goes to trial for treason against Elizabeth; is found guilty and sentenced to death.

1587 Executed on February 8.

1603 Elizabeth dies; James becomes James VI of Scotland and James I of England.

1612 Mary's body is moved to Westminster Abbey in London.

Mary's Family Trees

The = sign marks a marriage, with the | sign showing the children of that marriage underneath. Where one relative has been married more than once, the spouses are also numbered. Parents are indicated in bold. Children who later became parents are mentioned twice, once in italics and later in plain/bold type. The color red shows the closest relation to Mary Queen of Scots in each family tree.

Mary's French Relatives

Claude, Duke of Guise* = Antoinette de Bourbon*

|

1)	2)	3)	4)	5)	6)	7)	8)	9)	10)
Francis, Duke of Guise	Louise	Charles, Cardinal of Lorraine	Claud, Duke of Aumale	*Marie de Guise*	Louise, Bishop of Troyes	Antoinette, Abbess of Faremoutiers	Francis, Grand Prior General of the Galleys	Rene' Marquis d'Elboeuf	Renee' Abbess of St. Peter, Rheims

1. Louis, Duke of = Marie de Guise = 2. James V of Scotland
   Longueville

| | | | |
| | | | |

1)	2)		1)	2)	3)
Francis, Duke of Longueville	Louis (d. 1537)		James (d. 1541)	Robert (d. 1541)	MARY QUEEN OF SCOTS

* Claude and Antoinette have two other dead newborn sons.

Mary's Scottish Relatives

James IV of Scotland = Margaret Tudor

|

|

Janet Stewart,   *James V of*
Lady Fleming   *Scotland*
(illegitimate)

1. Princess Madeleine = James V of Scotland = 2. Marie de Guise

|

|

1)	2)	3)
James	Robert	**MARY QUEEN**
(d. 1541)	(d. 1541)	OF SCOTS

Mary's English Relatives

Henry VII of England = Elizabeth of York

|

|

1)
*Henry VIII of
England*

2)
Mary

3)
*Margaret
Tudor*

1. Catherine 2. Anne 3. Jane = Henry   Margaret Tudor = James IV
   of Aragon Boleyn Seymour VIII

Mary
Tudor   Elizabeth I   Edward VI   *James V of
Scotland*

Marie de Guise = James V
of Scotland

|

|

MARY QUEEN = Henry Stewart,
OF SCOTS   Lord Darnley

|

|

James VI of
Scotland

Principal Figures
in the Life of
Mary Queen of Scots

THE STUARTS

James V of Scotland—Mary's father, nephew of Henry VIII of England

James VI of Scotland and I of England—son of Mary Queen of Scots and Lord Darnley; he succeeded to the throne of England after Elizabeth's death

Stuart, Henry, Lord Darnley—Mary's second husband and step-second cousin, descendant of the royal houses of England and Scotland

Stewart, James, Earl of Moray—illegitimate son of James V, Mary's half-brother

THE GUISES AND THE FRENCH

Francis I of France—Henry II's father, Renaissance king
Francis II of France—Mary's childhood friend and first husband

Guise, Antoinette de—Mary's maternal grandmother, matriarch of the Guise family

Guise, Charles de, Cardinal of Lorraine—Mary's uncle and her mother's brother, prominent politician at French Court during King Henry II's reign

Guise, Francis, Duc de—Mary's favorite uncle on her mother's side; a military hero in France

Guise, Marie de—second wife of James V of Scotland and Mary's mother

Henry II of France—Mary's father-in-law after her marriage to his son, Francis

Medici, Catherine de'—Italian-born wife of Henry II and Mary's mother-in-law after her marriage to Francis

Parois, Madame de—Mary's governess in France

Poitiers, Diane de—King Henry's mistress and confidante

Valois Princesses Elizabeth, Claude and Marguerite—daughters of Henry II and Catherine de Medici

THE TUDORS AND THE ENGLISH

Aragon, Catherine of—Spanish-born first wife of Henry VIII, mother of Mary Tudor

Babington, Anthony—planned to rescue Mary from her English prison in 1586

Boleyn, Anne—English-born second wife of Henry VIII, mother of Elizabeth I of England

Cecil, William—Queen Elizabeth's secretary of state, considered Mary a threat to Elizabeth

Dudley, Robert, Earl of Leicester—Elizabeth I's lifelong confidant and favorite at Court, his name put forth by Elizabeth as a potential husband for Mary Queen of Scots

Hardwick, Bess of—Earl of Shrewsbury's wife, companion to Mary during the first ten years of her imprisonment

Henry VII of England—great-grandfather of Mary Queen of Scots, father of Henry VIII

Henry VIII of England—father of Mary Tudor and Elizabeth I
Knollys, Francis—Mary's first jailor in England

Norfolk, Duke of—chief judge at the Conference of York, wanted to marry Mary

Shrewsbury, Earl of—one of Mary's jailors in England

Throckmorton, Francis—cousin of Nicholas, in 1583 arrested on suspicion of aiding Mary

Throckmorton, Nicholas—Queen Elizabeth's special ambassador to Scotland and France

Edward—son of Henry VIII, Henry planned to marry Mary to Edward

Tudor, Elizabeth—Henry VIII's daughter who succeeded her

half-sister, Mary Tudor as Queen of England; the last of the Tudor monarchs, Mary Stuart's cousin

Tudor, Mary—daughter of Henry VIII and Catherine of Aragon, succeeded Henry VIII as Queen Mary of England

Walsingham, Francis—Elizabeth I's chief secretary, and spy.

THE LENNOX CLAN

Darnley, Lord Henry—son of the Earl of Lennox and Margaret Douglas, Mary's second husband

Lennox, Margaret, Countess of—mother of Lord Darnley, wife of Earl of Lennox

Lennox, Matthew, Earl of—Lord Darnley's father

THE SCOTS

Argyll, Earl of—royal descendant of James I of Scotland, cousin of Mary

Argyll, Jean Stewart, Countess of—confidant of the Queen of Scotland, wife of the earl of Argyll, present at the assassination of Riccio

Balfour, James—Lord Darnley's friend who betrayed him, owner of house where Darnley was assassinated

Beaton, David—Cardinal Archbishop of Scotland

Bothwell, James Hepburn, Earl of—Mary's third husband, soldier; loyal to the crown and Scotland

Gordon, Jean—Bothwell's first wife; sister to Huntly

Gordon, John—third son of the Earl of Huntly; executed by James Stuart, earl of Moray

Gordon, George Lord—Earl of Huntly's eldest son, sworn enemy of Mary's brother, James

Hamilton, James, Earl of Arran—great-grandson of James II of Scotland

Huntly, George, Earl of—held lands and power in the Highlands of the northeast of Scotland

Knox, John—a former priest, a leader of the Reformation in Scotland, an outspoken enemy of Mary Queen of Scots

Ruthven, Patrick, Lord—nobleman who took part in Riccio's murder, said to possess powers of witchcraft

Stewart, John of Traquair—captain of the queen's guard

OTHER FIGURES IN MARY'S LIFE

Don Carlos of Spain—heir to the Spanish throne, potential husband for Mary after Francis' death

Gifford, Gilbert—double agent, worked for Francis Walsingham

Nau, Charles—French-born surgeon who administered to Mary at Jedburgh, brother of Claude

Nau, Claude—French-born secretary during Mary's final years in England, brother of Charles

Philip II of Spain—father of Don Carlos

Preston, Simon—proprietor of Craigmillar Castle, trusted friend of the queen

Riccio, David—Italian-born private secretary to Mary, musician, confidant

Glossary

adieu: farewell

annul a marriage: to declare a marriage invalid

auld: Scottish word meaning "old"

Bourbon Dynasty: a ruling family of France

Calvinist: someone who follows the theological doctrine of John Calvin

château: castle

clan: group of people tracing descent from a common ancestor

crown matrimonial: title conferred by Parliament making the husband of the queen a king in his own right

dauphin: eldest son of a king of France; the heir to the throne

dauphine: wife of the dauphin

dowager queen: widowed queen holding the title from her deceased husband

dropsy: an excess accumulation of serous fluid in the body's connective tissues that causes considerable swelling and pain.

entourage: group of people that accompanies someone on a trip, etc.

feudal: a system where land was held by the lords and worked by the tenants who lived on the land

galley: a boat propelled chiefly by oars

Huguenots: French Protestants

in absentia: in absence (when a person is not present)

loch: lake (Scottish)

masque: form of entertainment, at times very extravagant

parliament: legislative body of government

Privy Council: advisory council to the king or queen

provost: administrative officer; an obsolete meaning referred to a prison warden

proxy: a marriage celebrated in the absence of the marriage bride or groom

purging: Sixteenth-century medical practice used to try to relieve a patient's pain

regent: someone who governs a kingdom until the rightful king or queen is old enough to rule

regicide: the killing of a king

rheumatism: a condition characterized by inflammation or pain in muscles, joints, or fibrous tissue

Stewart Dynasty: the ruling family of Scotland from which Mary Queen of Scots descended; when Mary arrived in France she changed the spelling to Stuart.

syphilis: a contagious venereal disease

to come of age: when a child king or queen becomes old enough to rule a country

tableaux: scenes, paintings

tribunal: court of justice

valet: male servant

Valois Dynasty: ruling family of France from which Francis (Mary's first husband) was descended.

Sources

CHAPTER ONE: Rough Wooing

p. 11-12 "It cam wi' a lass . . ." J. Keith Cheetham, *On the Trail of Mary, Queen of Scots* (Edinburgh: Luath Press Limited, 1999), 9.

p. 15, "auld enemie," Jane Dunn, *Elizabeth and Mary: Cousins, Rivals, Queens* (New York: Alfred A. Knopf, 2004), 62.

p. 15, "Who that intendeth France . . ." John Guy, *The True Life of Mary Queen of Scots* (Boston and New York: Houghton Mifflin Company, 2004) 14.

p. 18, "the most inconstant man," Ibid., 19.

p. 19, "it is as goodly a . . ." John MacLeod, *Dynasty: The Stuarts 1560-1807* (New York: St. Martin's Press, 1999), 35.

p. 21, "with such solemnity . . ." Dunn, *Elizabeth and Mary*, 61.

p. 21, "rough wooing," Antonia Fraser, *Mary, Queen of Scots* (New York: Delacorte Press, 1969), 22.

p. 21, "put all to fire . . ." Ibid., 62.

p. 24, "one of the most perfect . . ." Guy, *The True Life of Mary Queen of Scots,* 39.

CHAPTER TWO: Most Perfect Child
p. 26, "She is the prettiest . . ." Guy, *True Life of Mary*, 43.
p. 26, "She has auburn hair . . ." Ibid.
p. 27, "not even as clean . . ." Ibid.
p. 28, "walk ahead of my daughters . . ." Ibid., 44.
p. 29, "From the very first day . . ." Ibid., 45.
p. 29-30, "the most perfect child . . ." Alison Weir, *Mary, Queen of Scots and The Murder of Lord Darnley* (New York: Ballantine Books, 2003), 12.
p. 31, "I can assure you . . ." Dunn, *Elizabeth and Mary*, 95.
p. 32, "beautiful gardens!" Fraser, *Mary, Queen of Scots*, 46.
p. 32, "to win the heart . . ." Guy, *True Life of Mary*, 46.
p. 34, "become very wise . . ." Dunn, *Elizabeth and Mary*, 92.
p. 35, "already possessed of a high . . ." Guy, *True Life of Mary*, 59.
p. 35, "I see that you're afraid . . ." Ibid., 62.
p. 35, "Because I was afraid . . ." MacLeod, *Dynasty: The Stuarts*, 53.
p. 35, "I hear she is troubled . . ." Dunn, *Elizabeth and Mary*, 169.

CHAPTER THREE: Line of Succession
p. 46, "My subjects in Scotland . . ." Fraser, *Mary, Queen of Scots*, 101.
p. 46, "The Queen my good sister . . ." Ibid.

CHAPTER FOUR: Adieu, France!
p. 55, "Adieu, France!" Fraser, *Mary, Queen of Scots*, 131.
p. 59, "Highland mantles," Ibid., 185.
p. 59, "Only a lady of perfect . . ." Ibid., 186.

p. 62, "have their eyes fixed . . ." Ibid., 162.

p. 63, "This Queen wished . . ." Ibid., 167.

p. 63, "She has begun to . . ." Ibid., 224.

CHAPTER FIVE: Love and Murder

p. 66, "He was the properest . . ." Fraser, *Mary, Queen of Scots*, 223.

p. 67, "poor Queen whom . . ." Ibid., 227.

p. 72, "So shall they not . . ." Ibid., 247.

p. 72, "May it please your . . ." Cheetham, *On the Trail of Mary*, 83-84.

p. 73, "Great Offense!" Ibid., 83.

p. 73, "Lay not hands on me . . ." Fraser, *Mary, Queen of Scots*, 252.

p. 74, "Justice, justice . . ." Cheetham, *On the Trail of Mary*, 84.

p. 74, "No more tears now . . ." Ibid., 254.

p. 75, "Oh my brother, if . . ." Ibid., 256.

CHAPTER SIX: The Death of a King

p. 78, "high in his own conceit . . ." Fraser, *Mary, Queen of Scots*, 262.

p. 80, "Here I protest to . . ." Ibid., 268.

p. 80-81, "more than sixty . . . all her limbs," Ibid., 276.

p. 82, "I will that ye . . ." Guy, *True Life of Mary*, 299.

p. 83, "let the matter be . . ." Ibid., 272.

CHAPTER SEVEN: Most Changed Woman

p. 91-92, "people for the . . . not fear to touch," Guy, *True Life of Mary*, 299.

p. 94, "accompanied none the less . . ." Fraser, *Mary, Queen of Scots*, 316.

p. 95, "The opinion of many . . ." Guy, *True Life of Mary*, 324.

p. 96, "Judge and avenge my cause . . ." Fraser, *Mary, Queen of Scots*, 329.

p. 98, "Burn the Whore!" Dunn, *Elizabeth and Mary*, 307.

p. 99, "We assure you that . . ." Ibid.

CHAPTER EIGHT: No More Ado About Her

p. 104, "notable woman," Fraser, *Mary Queen of Scots*, 371.

p. 108, "bring the man . . ." Guy, *True Life of Mary*, 389.

p. 108, "some invention more secret . . ." Ibid., 401.

p. 108, "From Glasgow . . ." Fraser, *Mary, Queen of Scots*, 393.

p. 108, "worse than your uncle's . . ." Guy, *True Life of Mary*, 398.

p. 108, "marriage," Fraser, *Mary, Queen of Scots*, 399.

p. 108, "to the declaration . . ." Ibid., 408.

p. 109, "from Glasgow this Saturday morning," Ibid., 393.

p. 109, "I will live . . ." Guy, *True Life of Mary*, 448.

p. 109, "As you please command . . ." Ibid.

p. 111, "if ye strike not . . ." Will and Ariel Durant, *The Story of Civilization VII: The Age of Reason Begins* (New York: Simon and Schuster, 1961), 126.

p. 112, "cutting of the most . . ." Guy, *True Life of Mary*, 452.

p. 113, "cut off her head . . " Ibid., 455.

CHAPTER NINE: Captivity

p. 116, "In my end . . ." Cheetham, *On the Trail of Mary*, 7.

p. 116, "pattern of dresses . . ." Guy, *True Life of Mary*, 438.

p. 116, "She did set such . . ." Ibid., 427.

p. 119, "No one can cure . . ." Ibid., 433.

p. 125 "despatch of the usurping . . ." Ibid., 487.

p. 125, "retire out of this . . ." Fraser, *Mary, Queen of Scots,* 490.

p. 125 "a good army . . ." Ibid., 488.

p. 126, "Madame, the Queen . . ." Ibid., 493- 494.

CHAPTER TEN: A Queen Condemned

p. 127, "For myself, I am . . ." Fraser, *Mary, Queen of Scots,* 499.

p. 128, "I am a Queen . . ." Guy, *True Life of Mary*, 473.

p. 128, "Look to your consciences . . ." Fraser, *Mary, Queen of Scots*, 507.

p. 128, "theatre of the world . . ." Ibid., 507.

p. 129, "For my part, I . . ." Ibid., 513.

p. 129, "My advancing age . . ." Ibid., 511.

p. 130, "Ah! You are indeed . . ." Ibid., 515.

p. 130, "I desired nothing but . . ." Ibid.

p. 130, "My lords and gentlemen . . ." Ibid., 516.

p. 131, "I thank you for . . ." Ibid., 531.

p. 131, "permit my poor desolated . . ." Durant, *The Story of Civilization*, 129.

p. 135, "Into your hands . . ." Fraser, *Mary, Queen of Scots*, 539.

p. 136, "In my end . . ." Ibid., 555.

Bibliography

Adams, Simon. "Two Missing Lauderdale Letters. Queen Mary to Robert Dudley, Earl of Leicester, 5 June 1567 and Thomas Randolph and Francis Russell, Earl of Bedford to Leicester, 23 November 1564." *Scotland Historical Review* 70 (1991): 55–57.

Baring, Maurice. *In My End Is My Beginning*. New York: Alfred A. Knopf, 1931.

Basing, Patricia. "Robert Beale and the Queen of Scots." *The British Library Journal* 20 (1994): 65, 73-75.

Cheetham, J. Keith. *On the Trail Of Mary, Queen of Scots*. Edinburgh: Luath Press Limited, 1999.

Cowan, Ian B., ed. *The Enigma of Mary Stuart*. New York: St. Martin's Press, 1971.

Dunn, Jane. *Elizabeth and Mary: Cousins, Rivals, Queens*. New York: Alfred A. Knopf, New York, 2004.

Durant, Will and Ariel. *The Story of Civilization VII: The Age of Reason Begins*. New York: Simon and Schuster, 1961.

Fraser, Antonia. *King James VI of Scotland, I of England*. New York: Alfred A. Knopf, 1975.

———. *Mary Queen of Scots*. New York: Delacorte Press, 1969.

Guy, John. *The True Life of Mary Stuart, Queen of Scots*. Boston and New York: Houghton Mifflin Company, 2004.

Hopkins, Lisa. *Writing Renaissance Queens*. London: Associated United Presses, 2002.

Hurstfield, Joel, ed. *The Historical Association Book of The Tudors*. New York: St. Martin's Press, 1973.

King, Marian. *Young Mary Stuart, Queen of Scots.* Philadelphia and New York: J. B. Lippincott Company, 1954.

Lewis, Jayne Elizabeth. *Mary, Queen of Scots: Romance and Nation.* New York: Routledge Publisher,1998.

Linklater, Eric. *The Survival of Scotland: A New History of Scotland from Roman Times to the Present Day.* New York: Doubleday & Co., Inc., 1968.

Macleod, John. *Dynasty: The Stuarts 1560-1807.* New York: St. Martin's Press, 1999.

Miller, Joyce. *A Wee Guide to Mary, Queen of Scots.* Edinburgh: Goblinshead, 1996

Morrison, N. Brysson. *Mary, Queen of Scots.* New York: The Vanguard Press Inc., 1960.

de Peyster, J. Watts. *Mary Stuart, Bothwell, and the Casket Letters.* New York: Charles H. Ludwig, Printer, 1890.

Plaidy, Jean. *Mary, Queen of Scots: The Fair Devil of Scotland.* G. P. Putnam's Sons, Inc., 1975.

Prebble, John. *The Lion in the North.* New York: Coward, McCann & Geoghegan, Inc., 1971.

Shoemaker, Michael Myers. *Palaces and Prisons of Mary, Queen of Scots.* New York and London: G.P. Putnam's Sons, The Knickerbocker Press, 1903.

Singh, Simon. *The Code Book: The Evolution of Secrecy from Mary, Queen of Scots to Quantum Cryptography.* New York: Doubleday, 1999.

Stewart, Doug. "Reign On!" *The Smithsonian,* June 2003.

Thomson, George Malcolm. *The Crime of Mary Stuart.* New York: E. P. Dutton & Co., Inc., 1967.

Weir, Alison. *Mary, Queen of Scots and the Murder of Lord Darnley.* New York: Ballantine Books, 2003.

Web sites

http://www.marie-stuart.co.uk
On this site the Marie Stuart Society of Scotland provides a detailed biography, timeline, and family trees of Mary Queen of Scots, as well as information about her parents, husbands, childhood, captivity, letters, and lots of additional information, including images of her embroidery.

http://www.newadvent.org/cathen/09764a.htm
A detailed biography is featured on this site maintained by the Catholic Encyclopedia.

http://englishhistory.net/tudor/relative/maryqosbiography. html
This Web site includes an extensive biography, images, primary sources, Tudor quizzes, and other links for information about the life and times of Mary Stuart.

Index